HEART OF

ROMAN, MEDIE

REVEALED BY /

D0494259

A Description of London

Houses, churches, mixed together,
Streets unpleasant in all weather;
Prisons, palaces contiguous,
Gates, a bridge, the Thames irriguous.

Gaudy things enough to tempt ye,
Showy outsides, insides empty;
Bubbles, trades, mechanic arts,
Coaches, wheelbarrows and carts.

Warrants, bailiffs, bills unpaid,
Lords of laundresses afraid;
Rogues that nightly rob and shoot men,
Hangmen, aldermen and footmen.

Lawyers, poets, priests, physicians,
Noble, simple, all conditions:
Worth beneath a threadbare cover,
Villainy bedaubed all over.

Women black, red, fair and grey,
Prudes and such as never pray,
Handsome, ugly, noisy, still,
Some that will not, some that will.

Many a beau without a shilling,
Many a widow not unwilling;
Many a bargain, if you strike it:
This is London! How d'ye like it?

John Bancks (1738)

English tin-glazed earthenware pharmaceutical vessels from the 17th and 18th centuries, including ointment pots and drug jars

Heart of the City

Roman, medieval and modern London
revealed by archaeology at 1 Poultry

Peter Rowsome

ENGLISH HERITAGE

MUSEUM OF LONDON
Archaeology Service

First published in July 2000 by the
Museum of London Archaeology Service

© Museum of London 2000

A CIP catalogue record for this book is available from the British Library

ISBN 1 901992 14 4

English Heritage product code XD20026

**The research and writing of this book was generously
funded by English Heritage, who have also provided a
grant to cover the cost of publication**

Designed by Tracy Wellman, MoLAS

Edited by Monica Kendall

Reprographics by Andy Chopping, MoLAS

Printed in the UK by Linney Print
Mansfield, Notts NG18 4FL

One of the vessels from an
important group of unused samian
bowls, dishes and cups recovered
from a Roman shop destroyed in
the Boudican revolt of AD 60

Contents

An early
Roman
harness
pendant

Acknowledgements

This book is the result of the hard work and dedication of a large number of people and organisations. Analysis and publication of the findings from 1 Poultry have been generously funded by English Heritage. The archaeological excavation was funded by Lord Peter Palumbo's City Acre Property Investment Trust, with Dieter Bock and Advanta AG. Altstadtbau Limited, without whose help the results of the archaeological work would have been greatly diminished, managed the construction project.

Excavating the walls and mosaic floors of an unusual late Roman building found at Poultry

Many individuals and companies involved in the development at 1 Poultry deserve special thanks: Tim Carter and Eric Bruce of Altstadtbau, Laurence Bain and Andrew Pryke of Michael Wilford & Partners (architects), Don Armstrong-Smith and Lesley Baron of Armstrong Smith Baron, Ted Kear of John Laing Construction, Robert Pugh at Ove Arup and Partners (consulting engineers) and the staff of O'Rourke Civil Engineering. Colum McDonnell acted as John Laing Construction's archaeological liaison officer and did much to ensure that our excavations were a success, but passed away before he could see this book.

Staff at English Heritage making an important contribution to the work include Brian Kerr at the Centre for Archaeology, Tim Williams at Archaeology Commissions, Ellen Barnes at London Division, the former Chief Archaeologist Geoffrey Wainwright and the former Chairman Sir Jocelyn Stevens. Annie Hampson and Kathryn Stubbs of the Corporation of London Planning Department also played an important role in discussing the design of the archaeological programme.

The archaeological team from the Museum of London Archaeology Service was very large and it is not possible to mention everyone by name. Special thanks must go to the supervisory team of Mark Burch, Julian Hill, Sarah Jones, Duncan Lees, Adrian Miles and Phil Treveil, both for their efforts on site and the analysis and interpretation of the findings. Richenda Goffin was in charge of the finds work and Patrick Hunter of the environmental work. Andy Chopping, Margaret Cox and Ed Baker provided the site photography. MoLAS managers who played an important role in the project were Taryn Nixon and Richard Malt. This publication benefits from the hard work and insight of all those listed above.

Many other specialists have also made valuable contributions (Museum of London unless stated otherwise) and include Damian Goodburn (ancient woodwork), Ian Tyers (dendrochronology – University of Sheffield), Angela Wardle (Roman finds), Louise Rayner and Fiona Seeley (Roman pottery), Kevin Rielly and Alan Pipe (archaeozoology), Anne Davis and Lisa Gray-Rees (botany), David Smith (insect remains – University of Birmingham), Jane Corcoran (environmental archaeology at MoLAS), Jane Sidell (environmental archaeology – University College London), Rob Scaife (ancient pollen – University of Southampton), Richard Macphail (soil micromorphology – University College London), Lucy Whittingham (medieval pottery), Jacqui Keilly (leather), Geoff Egan (post-Roman finds), Patricia Reid (medieval leather shoes – University College London), Alison Nailer (post-Roman leather), Terry Smith (building material), Mark Samuel (worked stone), Bill White (human remains), Liz Goodman (conservation) and Justine Bayley and David Dungworth (metalworking – English Heritage Centre for Archaeology). Derek Keene of the Institute of Historical Research has carried out important documentary research into the Poultry area. David S Neal has analysed the Roman mosaics and provided reconstruction drawings of them. David Smith and David Peacock of the University of Southampton have analysed the Roman quernstones. Martin Millett of the University of Southampton and Vanessa Harding of Birkbeck College are academic advisers for the project and their guidance is greatly appreciated.

Other contributors to this book include Judith Dobie (reconstruction drawings of the Roman and medieval town – English Heritage Centre for Archaeology), Susan Banks (plans), Faith Pewtress (finds and animal drawings), Andy Chopping, Margaret Cox and Ed Baker (site and studio photography), Kate Pollard (terrain modelling), Su Lever (picture research), Jeremy Smith (prints and maps – Guildhall Library), Eva Yocum (photographic library), Tracy Wellman (compilation and layout), Ellen McAdam (internal editing) and Monica Kendall (copy and technical editing). Jenny Hall of the Museum of London has advised on the reconstruction of those Roman buildings from Poultry forming part of a Museum of London exhibition. Brian Kerr, Tim Williams and Ellen Barnes have commented on the draft text and Chris Sumner of English Heritage London Region has commented on chapters 10 and 11. Isabel Newth, Jenny Rowsome and Cathy Rowsome also read the draft and provided sound advice. Any mistakes or omissions which remain are the sole responsibility of the author.

An archaeologist examines the base of an early Roman timber-lined structure, found towards the end of the main excavation work

The sideplate from a Late Saxon bone-handled folding knife found at Poultry, with a geometric interlace panel showing a dog encircled by a double twisted cord

Recording late Roman buildings during the main phase of excavation at Poultry

Foreword
by Lord Palumbo

A civilised society is marked by the evidence it leaves of its creative energy, most particularly in the buildings of its time. The site of 1 Poultry contains the rich mulch from which the character and quality of the City of London can be distilled.

My association with the site began 42 years ago when I persuaded my father to invest in what was then a multi-owned mass of Victorian buildings with the Mappin & Webb building upon its eastward extreme. My dream was to acquire the whole site to place upon it a fit monument for the 20th century to complement George Dance at the Mansion House, Sir Edwin Lutyens at Midland Bank and Sir John Soane at the Bank of England.

Our first proposal, then known as 'Mansion House Square', would have created an open space in front of the Mansion House with an elegant building by Mies van der Rohe to the west. This was rejected in 1985. Sir James Stirling succeeded him and his design found favour. Development of the site ensured that its secrets were uncovered and the *genius loci* evoked. I am delighted that the Museum of London Archaeology Service is able in this volume to describe how that genius expressed itself in every generation in the development of the City of London.

Lord Palumbo of Walbrook

Introduction

This book tells the story of a remarkable archaeological site – a single patch of land on the bank of a small stream – which has been at the very heart of London for the last 2000 years. The exploration of the site has revealed people and events from the first days of London's founding by the Romans in about AD 47 right up to today. On the way our story takes in the changing fortunes of London – its growth into a Roman city, decline into ruin at the start of the 5th century, revival under King Alfred nearly 500 years later, medieval expansion to become Europe's pre-eminent centre, fire and plague, the world's wealthiest metropolis at the head of the British Empire, the Blitz and modern redevelopment.

In 1904 Niels Moeller Lund painted *The Heart of the Empire*. Looking west from the roof of the Royal Exchange to the Mappin & Webb building framed by the great junction of roads at Poultry and Queen Victoria Street thronged with traffic, with Mansion House to the left and St Paul's Cathedral in the background, the scene radiates a sense of being at the centre of things – to a Victorian the centre of the world. One of the people who believed the site was special was Lord Palumbo, whose goal of constructing a landmark building has now been achieved, although not without opposition. It seems that the Poultry site has always held a special place in our view of London, the junction of streets representing a focal point for the metropolis.

The sense of commitment to doing something out of the ordinary at Poultry led to a remarkable agreement between Sir Jocelyn Stevens of English Heritage and Lord Palumbo to jointly fund the archaeological work. This book celebrates the results of that work and looks at how archaeology can reveal aspects of history which cannot be discovered by any other means.

The Heart of the Empire, by Niels Moeller Lund, with the Mappin & Webb building framed by Poultry and Queen Victoria Street and St Paul's in the background

1 Digging up London – in theory and in practice

To remain ignorant of what happened before you were born is to remain always a child.

(Cicero, Roman orator and statesman, 106–43 BC)

Why Poultry?

An unusual copper-alloy balance with decorated weighing pans, balance beam and iron pointer. Over 800 Roman coins were found during the excavation

The Poultry site lies near the historic heart of the City of London – at the eastern end of Cheapside and near the Bank of England, the Mansion House and the Royal Exchange. The site covers part of what was once the western bank of the Walbrook – the small stream which ran through the Roman town to flow into the River Thames. The unusual name of the site – Poultry – is derived from the street along its north side which was known for its shops and businesses in the medieval period – particularly for its grocers and poulterers. One of London's largest ever archaeological excavations took place at Poultry between 1994 and 1996, a team of 50 archaeologists working away below ground level in what would become the basement levels in a new office building. This work was completely hidden from the public view even as tens of thousands of pedestrians passed overhead on their daily business.

London has developed from its Roman origins to become a modern capital that is a dynamic mixture of the old and the new. To a visitor London can seem a huge, complex and haphazard city and at first glance the strata on an archaeological site can appear similarly confusing. How is a modern, scientific archaeological excavation carried out and how can it take place at the same time as construction work? The answers are as much a part of this story as the findings themselves.

Use of a Roman balance

London is built on its thrown-away past

Within the City of London – the modern-day financial district – the physical residue of history has been accumulating for most of the last 2000 years. Nearly everything that people needed – from building stone and timber through to household goods and daily food supplies – was brought into the city by road or water. Until the 19th century very little of the rubbish was taken away. People buried their household waste in their backyards or tipped it on open ground. Whenever buildings burned down, fell down, or became dilapidated, the owners would salvage what was reusable, flatten out the demolished remains and build on top. At countless times throughout history people have resurfaced roads, filled in streambeds or reclaimed low-lying land. Contained within these layers is every sort of object – anything that was lost, broken or thrown away in the past. Nearly 42,000 fragments of Roman pottery and 54,000 animal bones were found during the Poultry excavation, and metal detectors were used by archaeologists to recover over 800 Roman coins.

As a result of these processes the ground surface has risen by a substantial amount in the City – an average of 3 or 4 metres, and as much as 8 metres within the Walbrook Valley, where Roman and medieval occupation was concentrated. These days all of London's waste is hauled away in trucks and tipped into huge landfill sites in the Thames estuary and elsewhere. As a result, London's ground surface has finally stopped rising. But the accumulation of layers of material associated with various events in history has formed an archaeological layer-cake beneath the City – one in which the lowest deposits are the earliest and the upper ones the most recent.

An archaeologist removing the contents of a small, early Roman pit which contained not only household rubbish but part of the base of a timber chest used for storing valuables

This cartoon shows Victorian buildings with shallow basements which partly cut into the archaeological sequence below, and how the deeper basement for a new building has caused more damage

A colourful layer-cake of thin floors inside a 12th-century building

What was found at Poultry?

Archaeological excavation involves the careful recording and removal of the accretions of history – one layer at a time and in the reverse order of their deposition: the latest first and the earliest last. If new buildings are designed to have bigger and deeper basements than past buildings in the same spot – as at Poultry – then an archaeological dig is essential, as the evidence would otherwise be destroyed without record. Nearly 20,000 archaeological layers were recorded and excavated at Poultry. Individual scale drawings were made of every archaeological structure and layer, using both pencil and paper and hand-held 'pen' computers. The location of all the deposits and structures was measured in relation to their height above sea level and position on the national map grid.

Making a detailed record of a Roman stone and tile wall along the south side of the main road at Poultry

Washing down a Late Saxon well in the environmental processing bay next to the site. The blue boxes contain soil samples to be sieved for environmental evidence such as seeds and fish bones

One of the best ways to find out how past Londoners lived is to study the animal bone and botanical remains they threw away. Bone was extremely well preserved by the wet soil conditions, with even fine surface details such as butchery marks and tooth wear clearly visible. The huge size of the assemblage includes many different species of animal, including some types never before found on London sites. Bone was collected by hand and also by washing over 1000 soil samples through nylon meshes of various sizes to retrieve everything from the smallest fish such as sprats and young eels, to large mammals like cattle and red deer. Residues from the soil samples were also examined for the remains of seeds and plants. Over 18,000 seeds, fruits, leaves and other plant parts have been found. Like the animal bones, these tell us about aspects of life in the past such as diet, trade and the economy and also the natural environment of the area.

By looking at the evidence from Poultry we have been able to identify the buildings that past Londoners lived in, the road surfaces they walked on and the pits where they threw their kitchen scraps or worse. A total of 73 Roman buildings, 84 yards and four roads have been found from the period AD 50–410. The medieval period up to the Great Fire in 1666 is represented by another 77 buildings, 52 yards and external areas and four roads. Evidence of the pre-Roman landscape and the post-medieval period has also been found. The excavation results add colour and detail to our understanding of the past, and allow the peopling of Roman, medieval and early modern London.

Reconstructing the past is the archaeologist's ultimate goal – such as in this reconstruction view of 1st-century Roman buildings and in the construction of full-scale replicas of buildings from Poultry for display at the Museum of London (left)

Aims of the dig

The Walbrook Valley has long been recognised as an area of outstanding archaeological survival and importance. Work on nearby sites in the 19th and 20th centuries resulted in several of London's most important archaeological discoveries, including a late Roman temple dedicated to Mithras. The Poultry site, with its shallow Victorian basements, was the last large site in the area where a deep archaeological sequence survived. Redevelopment only took place after a long and controversial planning battle, with permission to construct the new office building designed by James Stirling finally granted in 1989 by the Secretary of State for the Environment. The permission included a weak condition stating that 'The developer shall afford access at all reasonable times to any archaeologist nominated by the local planning authority, and shall allow him to observe the excavation and record items of interest and finds.'

This was not a requirement for full archaeological excavation and a crisis seemed likely. Lord Palumbo could have used heavy machinery to excavate the new basements and destroy the history of the site but this was not what he wanted. Instead he commissioned the Museum of London to carry out an Archaeological Assessment in December 1993, followed by archaeological evaluation work in April 1994.

The location of Poultry and some of the many other sites which have been excavated in the vicinity, superimposed on the modern street plan and also showing the course of the Walbrook stream. The numbered sites are referred to in the text: (1) 36 King Street, (2) 72 Cheapside, (3) Bucklersbury House, (4) St Swithin's House, (5) Bucklersbury DLR shaft, (6) National Safe Deposit Company, (7) Bucklersbury mosaic, (8) The Bank of England (9) Lothbury DLR shaft

The head of Mithras, discovered at Bucklersbury House in 1954

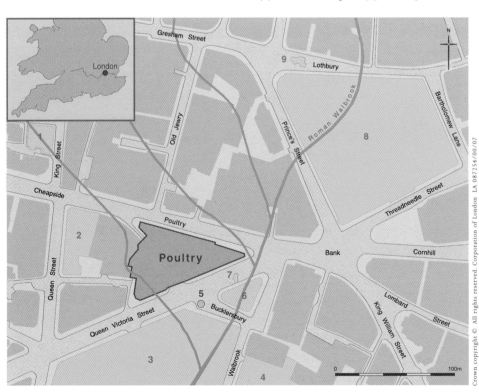

Evaluation work included sinking boreholes and excavating shafts within the basements of the Victorian buildings east of Bucklersbury. Complex deposits, including Roman and post-Roman buildings and structures, accompanied by excellent survival of environmental evidence, were found at all of the locations investigated. The assessment and evaluation work, coupled with the findings from neighbouring sites, was used to identify the requirements and research aims of the coming excavation. Aims included the study of the earliest Roman roads and buildings along the west side of the Walbrook stream, late Roman London and its abandonment at the end of the 4th century, the reoccupation of the city by King Alfred in the 9th century, the medieval City, and the lost church of St Benet Sherehog and its burial ground.

Everyone recognised the importance of the site but also how difficult it would be to provide the logistics required for full archaeological excavation. Poultry was not in a green field in the countryside but surrounded by streets, buildings and underground train tunnels which would all be at risk of movement once deep excavation began. A dig open to the sky would not be possible. No one had attempted such an ambitious and complicated marriage between archaeology, engineering and construction before.

On 7 June 1994 agreement was reached. In a press release on 8 June, Lord Palumbo said: 'this has been an exemplary case of the way in which heritage bodies and responsible developers can work together to achieve a common objective, namely a greater understanding of our heritage'.

A superbly preserved 1st-century bronze oil-lamp found during the evaluation work – the flame is simulated

An early Roman water pipe made from an oak log being recorded during the evaluation in 1994

Top-down construction and archaeology

Top-down construction refers to the construction of a new building's superstructure at the same time as the excavation of its basements. At Poultry the main foundation works for the new building were put in place before the start of the excavations, which would eventually create a hole measuring about 100 metres long and up to 60 metres wide, with a base 14 metres below the modern street level. Even the solid concrete and steel columns around the sides of the excavation would 'banana' (distort) at such depths unless braced from the inside, and this bracing was achieved by constructing the three basement floor levels in reverse order as the digging progressed.

A giant corkscrew into London's history: installing the main piled foundations for the new building – 74 concrete columns which extended 55 metres down into the underlying clay and chalk geology

A cross-section showing the archaeological sequence recorded at Poultry and the outline of the new building above. Archaeological excavation and construction of the new offices took place at the same time

The main phase of archaeological work took place after installation of a watertight perimeter wall, which can be seen in the background

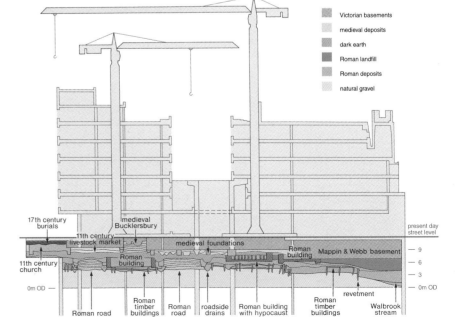

Victorian basements
medieval deposits
dark earth
Roman landfill
Roman deposits
natural gravel

17th century burials
medieval Bucklersbury
11th century livestock market
medieval foundations
Roman building
Mappin & Webb basement
present day street level
11th century church
Roman building
11th century church
Roman building with hypocaust
Roman timber buildings
revetment
Walbrook stream
0m OD
Roman road
Roman timber buildings
Roman road
roadside drains
Roman building with hypocaust
Roman timber buildings
Walbrook stream
— 9
— 6
— 3
— 0m OD

The archaeological dig took place in three phases fitted around the construction work. In the summer and autumn of 1994 archaeologists investigated the burial ground and church of St Benet Sherehog and the medieval streets of Bucklersbury and Pancras Lane while the new perimeter wall was being built. The main phase of archaeological work began in July 1995 and lasted for nine months. Investigation of the west bank of the Walbrook stream at the site apex involved digging to an even greater depth.

In July 1996 the Stirling building was 'topped-out' (completed to its full height), and the archaeological work finished on schedule, proving that archaeology and construction could coexist given the right conditions and cooperative effort.

Archaeological life below the slab – the vertical beams carry the weight of the new building as construction progresses

Contrary to the popular belief that the only tools an archaeologist needs on a dig are a trowel and fine brushes, a wide range of equipment was used at Poultry and included a ventilation system, specialist film-studio lighting and electric pumps to dewater the ground. Digging was aided by the use of conveyor belts and 360-degree excavators for moving earth, which was taken to 'moling-holes' (gaps in the ceiling), where it was lifted into trucks on a temporary vehicle bridge. Two tower cranes were sometimes used to lift heavy objects such as ancient timbers.

Constructing the ground-floor slab for the new building before beginning the dig: this helped to brace the sides of the site and allowed archaeologists to work in safety beneath the construction work

2 A green and pleas-ant land?

up to AD 43

It is difficult to imagine the area of central London as a rural idyll when we look at it today. It seems surprising that this piece of expensive real estate remained almost entirely unoccupied up until the Romans arrived in Britain just after AD 43, given the economic and strategic importance that has been attached to this place ever since. Pre-Roman Britain was neither empty nor entirely uncivilised, but so far as we can tell there was no significant settlement at London.

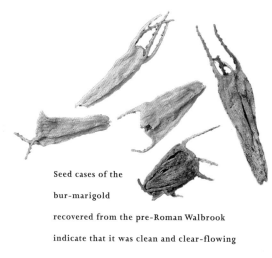

Seed cases of the bur-marigold recovered from the pre-Roman Walbrook indicate that it was clean and clear-flowing

London sits on a thick deposit of clay sediment dating from many millions of years ago when a deep sea occupied this part of the globe. Over the last half million years or so – between stages of the Ice Age – the River Thames has repeatedly formed a floodplain across the London area, depositing layers of clean sand and gravel each time. Flint tools used by early man, who hunted in the region over a quarter million years ago, are sometimes found within these gravels. There were times when the area lay to the south of the retreating ice and enjoyed a mild climate, with plentiful wildlife similar to that now found in Africa. After the end of the last Ice Age, in about 8000 BC, there would certainly have been hunting camps around the Thames but these have left little trace. Farming probably began to appear in about 4000 BC, and close to the river, woodland clearance for agriculture intensified during the Bronze Age (3000–600 BC), when the Thames is known to have been both a trade route and a sacred site. But the area of the City remained empty.

Research has shown that the Walbrook stream looked like this before the Romans arrived just after AD 43

14

At Poultry an ancient soil horizon survived above the sand and gravel. Pollen found within these deposits indicates that the area supported lime forest in the Bronze Age but had been partly cleared of trees before the Romans arrived – although no evidence of Iron Age occupation (600 BC–AD 43) was found at the site despite a situation which would seem perfect for farming, fishing and hunting and gathering – lying on the slope of the western of two low hills on the north side of the Thames, adjacent to the Walbrook stream. This hillside was crossed by small tributary streams fed by natural springs. The land was clothed by a mixture of open oak and hazel woodland with bracken undergrowth and damp grassy clearings on the slopes, and marshy alder carr in flatter areas and along the streams. Environmental samples show that the Walbrook was clean and clear-flowing and did not dry up in the summers, supporting aquatic plants, insects and freshwater molluscs.

A computer-generated model of the terrain at Poultry showing the position of the Walbrook and its tributaries. The site boundaries and position of the later Roman road crossing are highlighted

The south-east part of Iron Age Britain was quite populous, with powerful tribal kingdoms to both the north and south of the Thames. These people were not barbarous – although it suited the Romans to say that they were. In fact extensive trade and diplomatic links had been developing between Britain and the Romans ever since Julius Caesar's failed invasion attempt a century earlier, in 54 BC, and some of the tribes had even entered into formal treaties and alliances with Rome.

Forest clearance and farming had already begun to change the appearance of the London area by the Bronze Age

3 A Roman frontier town

AD 43 to AD 125

Invasion

Coins of Claudius (AD 41–54) and Vespasian (AD 69–79) found at 1 Poultry

In AD 43 the Romans, under the Emperor Claudius, invaded Britain. The decision to cross the Channel may have been prompted by a desire to gain Claudius prestige at Rome and to interfere in British affairs. According to the historian and Roman consul Cassius Dio, writing about the invasion of Britain 150 years later, a large expeditionary force was assembled and included elephants. The south-eastern part of Britain was rapidly overrun despite stiff resistance.

Roman London in about AD 60, looking south-east towards the Thames, which was at that time wide and shallow compared to today. A ferry crossing probably preceded construction of a timber bridge

The Roman military realised the strategic importance of the Thames at London, which was at that time broad and shallow, with low sandy islands along its south side and no tide upstream of present-day London Bridge. Dio describes the situation at what would soon become London:

> The Britons now fell back on the River Thames, at a point near where it enters the sea, and at high tide forms a pool. They crossed over easily because they knew where to find firm ground and easy passage. But the Romans in trying to follow them were not so successful. However, the Germans again swam across, and other troops got over by a bridge a little upstream, after which they attacked the barbarians from several sides at once, and killed many of their number.

Within a year, Roman control of the south-east had been consolidated, although military campaigns spreading north and west were protracted, and Wales and Scotland were never subjugated.

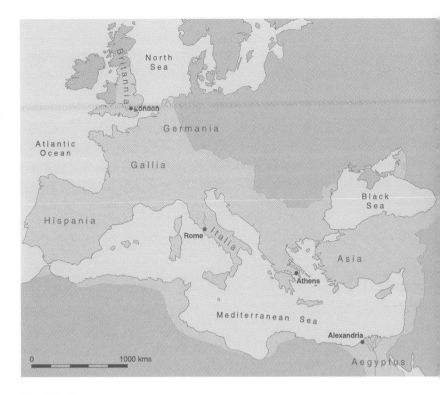

Map of the Roman Empire – London and Britain were far from the centres of Roman civilisation

A selection of flat, circular copper-alloy studs from the mid to late 1st century. Some may be from military equipment

A post-and-plank revetment along the south side of the new Roman road. Dendrochronological-dating of timbers from these structures and from small drains contemporary with the road has shown that some were cut in AD 47 – could this be the year that London was founded?

The founding of Londinium

The limit of the tidal reach and the presence of two low hills on the north bank of the Thames made the City an obvious place to establish a permanent river crossing and a settlement. London could serve as a port and also as the centre for a road network radiating out across the new province. As a supply base or centre of trade it need not have been specifically civilian or military.

The east–west road was flanked by timber box-drains made from oak planks

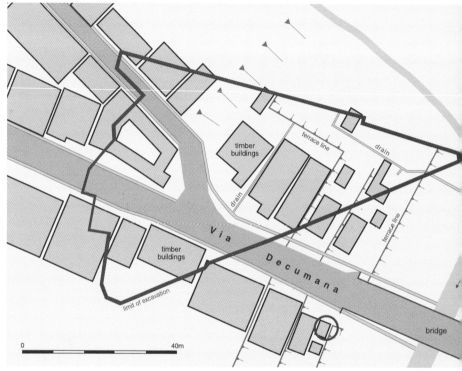

The layout of streets and buildings at Poultry just before AD 60, when London was already a thriving frontier town. A computer-generated image of this plan has been used as the basis for the artist's reconstruction on the facing page

At Poultry it has been possible to accurately date many of the ancient timbers using a method called dendrochronology (tree-ring-dating). Comparison of the varying width of annual growth rings allows the matching of trees growing in the same climatic conditions and comparison to a dated reference sequence. If the outer rings and bark are present on a sample then the exact felling date of the tree can be identified. The Romans did not season their oak but used it green, so the felling date can pinpoint construction dates to within a few weeks or months.

The earliest evidence of a Roman presence at Poultry is the construction of the town's main east–west aligned road (Via Decumana), which continued westwards to join the road system leading to the towns of Calleva (Silchester) and Verulamium (St Albans), and east to Camulodunum (Colchester). The Via Decumana was one of two principal roads within the new town. It intersected with the road which led from the south and crossed the River Thames to form a T-junction in front of what would later be the Roman forum beneath present-day Cornhill.

Archaeologists digging at Poultry discovered a long stretch of the east–west road, just to the west of the point at which it bridged the Walbrook, to the north of the tidal portion of the stream. Once across the Walbrook the road diverged slightly towards the north-west – to gain better, higher ground and avoid tributary streams – before crossing the Fleet River to the west of the settlement. A timber drain found beneath the earliest surface of the road at Poultry has been dated by dendrochronology to AD 47. This is five years older than the oldest precisely dated structure previously discovered in Roman London, and the best evidence yet for the likely date of London's founding.

The successful establishment of an entirely new town involves not just the construction of roads and infrastructure, but significant modification of the terrain through landscaping and drainage – and this remains as true today as it was 2000 years ago. The Romans had considerable expertise at town-building and this can be seen at Poultry, where a series of horizontal terraces was cut into the naturally sloping ground to the north of the new road. The soggy, low-lying areas to the south were criss-crossed by post-and-plank revetments, dating to AD 47/48, and sealed by landfill which prepared the area for housing development.

A 1st-century strap mount, probably from a belt

A reconstruction view looking north-west across the Walbrook stream shows just how quickly the new Roman town had grown by AD 60. Both the main road and narrow, secondary road were lined with timber buildings which included the houses, shops and industrial premises of a successful and busy frontier town

A timber building constructed in about AD 55 lay on the south side of the main road, just west of the Walbrook crossing. Timber partitions, doorways and a roadside boardwalk had all survived intact in the wet conditions

The primary surface of the main Roman road at Poultry was formed of rammed gravel laid on a raised roadbed of sand and clay/silt. The road was certainly wide enough for two carts to pass, and was flanked by timber box-drains made of oak planking with close-fitting lids. The roadside drains carried surface run-off east to the Walbrook stream, whose banks were straightened and retained with new timber revetments.

Shortly after the construction of the main road a narrow secondary road leading north-westwards was established on the western part of the site at Poultry, the two roads forming an odd, offset junction. Earth-and-timber buildings occupied most of the road frontages at Poultry by AD 60, with sheds and outhouses constructed on the land behind them. Backyards were criss-crossed by timber drains and apparently used by light industry and manufacturing. Everything was built or made of timber – high-quality oak was plentiful, while the nearest stone suitable for building had to be quarried in Kent, barged down the Medway and then up the Thames. The new buildings were rectilinear, timber-framed structures – the product of carpentry techniques introduced by the Romans such as sawing, prefabrication of parts and the use of a variety of joints and nails.

A narrow secondary road dating from Roman London's first years

London's strategic and economic importance as a port and road hub meant that it grew rapidly

The streets of the new town had a busy, mixed commercial and residential character. Used and broken millstones and raised, post-built structures were excavated at Poultry, and show that mills, bakeries and granaries – essential elements of a town's economy – had been established around the Walbrook crossing during the AD 50s. Study of environmental samples from some of the early buildings has revealed the presence of species of beetle such as the granary weevil, which feed on stored grain just as it begins to spoil. These creatures only appear in Britain after AD 43, when the Romans began importing large amounts of grain from the east Mediterranean and stored it above ground.

Early London may have been characterised by a very mixed population attracted by an opportunistic trading economy. The first settlers at Poultry were probably merchants, agents involved in the supply of the military, public officials and those attracted by rumours of money to be made. The town grew extremely quickly and was the largest town in the new province by AD 60, its growth fuelled by its importance as a port of entry for both goods and people. According to the great Roman historian Tacitus, London in AD 60 was 'not dignified by the title of colonia [an officially chartered town of Roman citizens such as Colchester], but abounded with dealers and was a celebrated centre for supplies'.

Once upon a time in the west

Is it possible that American frontier towns and early Roman London had a lot in common? The Kansas cattle towns of Abilene, Dodge City and Wichita were founded in the 1860s and 1870s by 'town-builders' – ambitious traders and speculators who identified strategically important points where the Texas Cattle Trails had to cross major rivers to intersect with the new railways approaching from the east. Town sites were surveyed and then actively promoted to attract settlers – military garrisons and the railways followed – and geographical advantage was turned into urban prosperity. The first traders from Gaul and settlers from elsewhere in Britain arriving in London in about AD 50 may have had remarkably similar motivations. Where conditions proved favourable the new towns experienced rapid growth and success – both on the American and the Roman frontier.

The three photographs below show Wichita, Kansas – top: view along Main Street in 1870 when the town was only two years old and consisted of a few rudimentary buildings and wagons; centre: bird's-eye view of the town in 1873 with a gridded street layout, over 2000 permanent residents, a railway and bridge; and bottom: same view of Main Street as top but in 1875 and with substantial business premises now established. Compare this pattern of development with that of London up to AD 60 and see what you think.

Cavalry-harness pendants are evidence for a military presence in London in the 1st century

Finds recovered from the earliest Roman layers at Poultry included military items such as fragments of armour, studs, belts and some weapons. The presence of soldiers at such an early date – when Britain was barely pacified – is hardly surprising, but it is uncertain exactly where they were based. Most of the early brooches found at Poultry may also be military types and it is interesting that the overall assemblage of early artefacts includes very little 'feminine' jewellery, suggesting that the early town was either predominantly male, as one might expect of a frontier town, or that the men of Londinium had taken up Roman fashions much more than the women.

Many of the timber buildings excavated at Poultry had been constructed in AD 58 and AD 59 – showing that 10 years after its founding the new town's growth was accelerating. One of the excavated buildings on the north side of the main road was apparently a shop selling household goods and supplies, including pottery from southern and central Gaul. A cache of charred spices was found in one of the rooms and included mustard, dill and fennel, with some coriander and black cumin – all used in Roman cooking. Small wooden spoons lying nearby may have been used for measuring out the spices.

Glazed-ware bowls from central Gaul formed part of the stock of the early Roman shop

The growth of London in the AD 50s must have had a huge impact on south-east Britain. A new town had been carved out of the landscape: forest cover and topsoil were removed from large areas, hillsides flattened and valleys infilled. The raw new townscape was prone to erosion and the Walbrook stream became a muddy, silt-laden channel subject to flash floods. More tellingly, the lives and livelihoods of the native population were disrupted by London's growth, even though the Romans would have tried to support the economic interests of tribal leaders and elites in order to gain their support. The Romans argued that the Pax Romana (Roman peace) brought prosperity and civilisation to conquered peoples, but a hatred of Rome smouldered beneath the surface calm of south-east Britain. One of the most famous quotes in Latin literature, which Tacitus attributes to a British tribal chief, sums up the Celtic view of the Romans: 'They rob, butcher, plunder, and call it "empire"; and where they make a desolation, they call it "peace".'

The author recording the chevron-decorated walls of a roadside shop which sold household goods in the AD 50s

Carbonised seeds identified as herbs had been spilled across the scorched brickearth floor of the shop, along with several small wooden spoons and wooden beads from a necklace

The Britons revolt against Rome

In AD 60 the British dislike of their new rulers boiled over as Boudica (Boadicea), the Queen of the Iceni of East Anglia, led a serious and bloody revolt against Rome which may have been prompted by overzealous taxation and enslavement. Tacitus tells us that the Roman towns in the destructive path of the rebels were evacuated, and we know that the new town was burned to the ground. Buildings at Poultry which were less than a year old were destroyed, and anyone who had remained behind was put to the sword or crucified. The Roman legions hurriedly returned from the Welsh frontier and inflicted a heavy defeat on the rebels somewhere north-west of London. Boudica poisoned herself and died.

At Poultry evidence of the revolt was clearly visible to archaeologists as a horizon of burnt debris overlying the ruins of the early buildings, some with their scorched timbers still in place. A deposit of soil and charcoal sealing the earliest metallings of the secondary road indicated a short period of disuse in the aftermath of the rebellion – civilians may have been reluctant to return to the town until absolutely certain that the army had restored security. The removal of any debris and reopening of the roads, particularly the main road, must have been a priority, but this was not accompanied by immediate rebuilding of roadside properties, which were at first merely tidied up. At the same time a new timber bridge over the Walbrook may have been built immediately to the north of the original bridge, which had been damaged or destroyed in the revolt. After a short hiatus London bounced back to become the foremost commercial centre in the Roman province, and the financial and administrative centre where the procurator was based – a high official directly responsible to the emperor in Rome for the economy of the province.

Boudica attacked and destroyed London in AD 60, but there is no archaeologiocal evidence that many people were killed and the population probably fled before she arrived

Londinium rebuilt

Londinium was rebuilt on a more ambitious scale. At Poultry new roads were established leading north towards the Upper Walbrook and south to the Thames. The road junction had now become a proper crossroads, and the north-west route was resurfaced. In all, parts of five new insulae (city blocks) were identified within the excavation area, each containing successive phases of roadside timber buildings dating from about AD 70 onwards. The new buildings included a greater variety of materials and styles of construction than their predecessors, and were set more closely together than before, but generally reflected the alignments and plot boundaries of the buildings they replaced — showing that property records and descriptions put in place before the revolt had been maintained.

Archaeologists recording the massive oak beams of a new building dating from about AD 70. The rebuilding of Londinium after the revolt sent a message that the Romans were determined to stay

The layout of streets and buildings at Poultry in about AD 100, when the Roman town's development and population was nearing a peak, also shown as an artist's reconstruction opposite

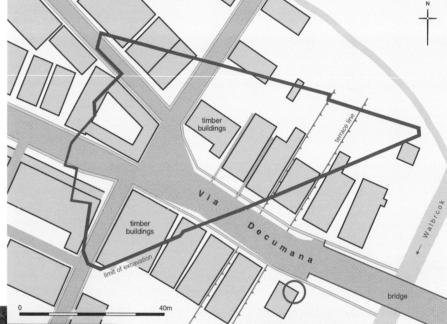

A 1st-century copper seal box with an appliqué frog on the lid. The frog was an attribute of the god Sabazios and considered a good-luck symbol

Rare evidence of early Roman building timbers with complex joints was recovered from the later roadside drains. The timbers had been sharpened and reused as driven posts to support the plank sides of the drains

Excavation of a small drain in an alley between two late 1st-century buildings north of the main road

A reconstruction view looking north across the site in about AD 100 and showing the town at its most populous. The main road is now joined by roads leading north-west, north and south. Timber buildings and yards occupy all the available ground and the frontier town has become a prosperous city

Five adjacent late 1st-century roadside properties were excavated along part of the north side of the main road, east of the road junction. These buildings had relatively narrow road frontages which probably contained shops, with corridors and interconnecting small rooms towards the back. Eavesdrips and covered drains between the properties carried rainwater south and into a larger roadside drain, which may also have been covered.

Relief from Ostia in Italy showing a vegetable stall with goods set out for sale. In London regular markets were probably held at the forum and along some of the main streets, perhaps run from shops incorporated into the fronts of roadside buildings

Houses and shops in Herculaneum, destroyed by the eruption of Vesuvius in AD 79. London also became densely built up, at least along the major roads such as the Via Decumana

Coin from the reign of the Emperor Vespasian (AD 69–79)

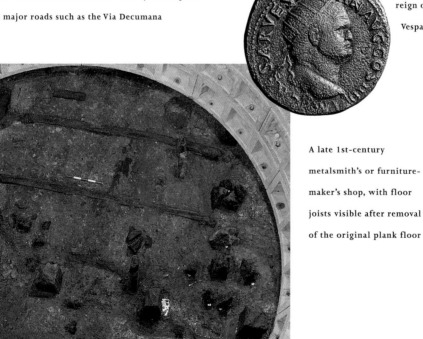

A late 1st-century metalsmith's or furniture-maker's shop, with floor joists visible after removal of the original plank floor

Metalwork, such as this military cavalry-harness pendant, had been lost through the cracks in the floor

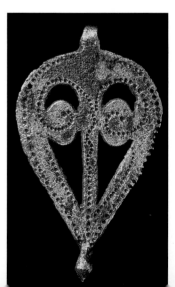

One of the buildings was constructed on a large platform of oak beams dated to after AD 73. The building may have been a bakery, and contained a central corridor with rooms to either side where grain had been scattered across the floors. Deposits of cereal bran suggest that wholemeal flour was being sieved to make higher-quality white flour. An oval, wooden trough for kneading dough was found behind the building. A variety of mealworm beetles found in deposits from the building normally feed on decaying flour, and are species one would expect to see in sweepings from storehouses and shops.

The excavation of a double-oven, possibly evidence of a bakery, dating to the late 1st century

A reconstruction of a double oven in a bakery and hot food shop, as found at Poultry

Small round-bowled spoons may have been used in either homes or shops to measure out small quantities of valuable herbs and spices

A 1st-century well constructed from reused silver-fir barrels. The lower barrel was recovered complete

A neighbouring building also contained several small rooms as well as a backyard shed around a water reservoir built from reused silver-fir barrels. Offcuts of silver fir and other timberwork suggest that a carpenter may have used the building. Buildings to the south of the road included a jeweller or furniture-maker. All of the roadside buildings may have incorporated roadside stalls or shops, which may have been run by the property-owners or rented out as separate units.

Detail showing the branded stamp CEGFIC across the barrel's bung and perhaps intended to prevent tampering during shipment. The barrel was originally used to import wine to London from the German frontier

Unlike many large Roman towns, Londinium probably did not need an aqueduct to supply fresh water to its inhabitants, as a copious supply of clean, fresh water was readily available from spring lines or from the sand and gravel beds which lay just below the surface and could be tapped by sinking timber-lined wells, many of which were excavated at Poultry. The Walbrook may have been a source of usable water in the town's very early years, but the stream quickly became polluted by surface run-off and industry.

Relief from Trajan's Column showing similar barrels being delivered by boat to a military base

A 1st-century copper-alloy plate brooch in the form of three men in a boat, with the prow taking the form of a bird. The brooch was probably from the Continent and may have been decorative but could also have had religious connotations

A Roman honey pot which had been dropped into a well, probably by accident

The land to the north of the roadside buildings and extending east to the Walbrook stream was used for light industrial activities and water extraction and storage. A clay lined and oak-planked water-tank with a capacity of about 2000 gallons was connected to a supply channel and an overflow pipe, and may have been part of a fulling and dyeing mill where spun cloth was sent for treatment. Fulling was an important Roman industry carried out by the *coactiliarii*, who trod the finished cloth in a mixture of fuller's earth, potash, soda and urine. The cloth was then rinsed and dried, brushed and either colourfully dyed or bleached before sale.

An amphora found in the disused water-tank came from the Cadiz region in southern Spain and had been used to transport garum and muria, fermented fish sauces used in Roman cuisine. Five lines of painted inscription or tituli picti on the neck refer to the contents and their origin and weight

A timber trough uncovered on the west bank of the Walbrook stream and originally used in light-industrial or processing work

The wooden frame and waterproof clay lining of the water-tank after removal of the planking

Just a few of the 1100 rotary quernstones recovered from the 1st-century yard, the largest assemblage to be studied from anywhere in the Roman Empire. The majority were made of lava and had been imported from Germany. Wear patterns indicate that the querns had been used prior to disposal, probably in a nearby mill or bakery

One of Londinium's best-preserved timber buildings lay just to the south of the tank. The yard around the tank and building was surfaced with broken millstones. Not everything about the town was well organised and tidy, though. Analysis of soil samples collected from the yards behind the roadside buildings has revealed large numbers of housefly and horsefly pupae associated with kitchen waste and other domestic rubbish. Pigs, chickens and other animals were kept in the yards and outbuildings, and the presence of dungheaps added to the squalid conditions. Botanical evidence from the yards includes a variety of weeds such as thistles and stinging nettles.

Roman technology was capable of producing high-quality glass vessels and many different types were imported to London, such as these handles and other fragmnents

One of 1st-century London's best-preserved timber buildings was discovered at Poultry. It contained rare evidence of collapsed partitions and a door

Roman knife handle with lion's head decoration

The findings at Poultry confirm that the population and wealth of Roman London grew markedly during the late 1st century. To the Romans, a proper town was not only a symbol of civilisation but also an important instrument in the introduction of Roman customs in far-flung parts of the empire. Londinium was provided with visually impressive monumental public buildings – the forum-basilica (which functioned as court, town hall and market), a sophisticated public baths, an amphitheatre which could seat 8000 spectators and extensive new port facilities. Some of these buildings were grandiose – perhaps even 'white elephants', but the town would continue to prosper until a second major fire caused widespread destruction in about AD 125.

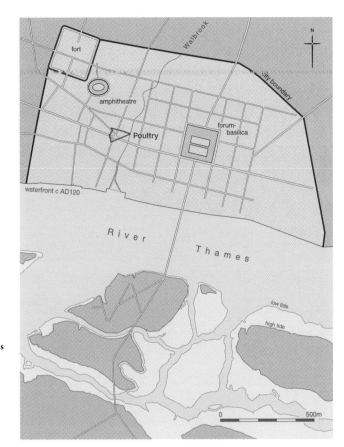

Plan showing the extent of early
2nd-century development of the
Roman town north of the Thames
and the low islands to the south

Roman London in the early 2nd century, looking north-west.
The Thames has been bridged, and the amphitheatre, fort and
public baths have been constructed west of the Walbrook

4 Daily life in Londinium in AD 100

AD 100

The people

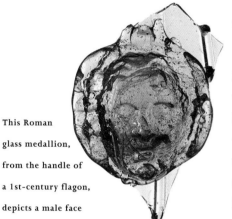

This Roman glass medallion, from the handle of a 1st-century flagon, depicts a male face

It would be fascinating to know what it was like to live in a Roman town and the variety of evidence which exists from sites like Poultry, Italy itself and in classical literature allows us to try to reconstruct the past. We know that early Roman London was the home of a cosmopolitan mixture of people from Britain and the Continent, many of them attracted by the opportunities offered by life in a new frontier town – and no doubt included veterans, officials and traders. Prosperous Roman citizens would have been present, some from Italy and far-flung parts of the Empire, but there were also freedmen, slaves and the urban poor.

A baker and his wife, from a Pompeiian wall painting. The woman would have played an important role in running the business and she holds a stylus and writing tablet for drawing up the accounts

A mixture of slaves and freedmen – whose livelihood depended on their muscle power – probably carried out much of the heavy work in the port, mills, tanneries and other industries, and were also employed as domestic servants. Londinium also included craftspeople, who prospered according to the skill of their hands, and a large and varied 'service sector' which relied on its ability to make a sale or close a deal. Because of its port, London was an emporium and there was money to be made both directly from trade and from associated activities such as transport, storage and tax collection.

It is not easy to estimate the size of the population but it may have been as great as 5–10,000 by AD 60, and probably peaked at 20,000 or so in the early 2nd century. Half of those born probably died before reaching adulthood, so the population structure would have been very different from what we are used to today. About a quarter of the population may have made it to old age – above the age of 40 – showing that longevity was quite good for those who survived childhood. Roman society venerated old men. Unfortunately, of all these people – young or old – we know the names and personal details of only a handful of individual Roman Londoners.

A depiction of a 2nd-century metalworker's shop, from Naples. Similar metalworking must have been taking place in the Walbrook Valley at the same time

A moulded face on the shoulder of a jar, an unusual piece which appears to be of Romano-British manufacture

The main Roman road at Poultry would have been a busy thoroughfare, used by Londoners and visitors going about their daily business – the equivalent of the High Street in an English town today

Inside the home

The homes and businesses of late 1st-century Londoners who lived at Poultry were located in single-storey, timber-framed buildings. Walls were made of compressed earth, mudbrick, or lathe and plaster. Exteriors may have been whitewashed or weatherboarded. Roofs were sometimes thatched, although most were made of overlapping boards or wooden shingles. Businesses such as bakeries, metalworking and craft shops were well established in the rooms and backyards of these roadside houses, with activities requiring a greater use of water clustering in the Walbrook Valley. Unlike modern towns, the Roman town was generally not formally divided into residential, commercial and industrial zones, or into separate quarters for the rich and the poor, and the presence of noxious industries and farm animals in close proximity to living quarters would have made town-life insalubrious. Unwelcome guests in the Roman households at Poultry included the house mouse and black rat.

Reconstruction of one of the timber buildings excavated at Poultry, showing the framing, roof construction and wall with window

Full-scale replica of one of the late 1st-century Roman buildings from Poultry, under construction for display in an exhibition at the Museum of London

Asterix in Britain gives us another example of how Roman London can be reconstructed. Here Asterix and Obelix arrive in Londinium but have some difficulty finding No. LVII as all the houses along the main street are near identical thatched cottages

Part of an early 2nd-century building excavated at 36 King Street to the north-west of Poultry. Substantial buildings with tessellated floors were built along the secondary streets as the Roman town grew

Many of the owners, shopkeepers and workers from the buildings uncovered at Poultry must have lived and slept on the premises or rented single rooms nearby. Life would have been austere. Very few houses had their own bathing or toilet facilities – human waste was either carted away, dumped in backyards, or tipped into roadside drains or the Walbrook stream. Workrooms, bedrooms and storerooms within the buildings were tiny, although the lofts and roof spaces may also have been used. The interiors of the buildings were sparsely furnished and modestly decorated, with beaten earth or plain mortar floors and the occasional black-and-white mosaic pavement. Shutters would have allowed in some light but most rooms were dark and dingy. Evidence for the positioning of oil-lamps suggests that people sometimes worked either at floor level or on raised benches, but detailed jobs requiring good light presumably took place in outbuildings which were less enclosed. Glazed windows and underfloor heating, although available in the public baths, were probably unheard of in priva homes in the 1st century, and in the winter daily life could be cold, damp and miserable. For a native of Italy, two weeks' hard-travelling away from his native land, Britain must have sometimes felt like the ends of the earth.

Roman Londoners lit their homes with oil-lamps such as this one from Poultry. The chains and hook allowed the lamp to be carried about and hung from existing fittings or from wall studs – as shown on page 11

The most complete Roman door ever found in London had been reused as an area of flooring in a 1st-century building

Drawing of the door showing the three boards which were planed and rebated to keep out the weather and held together by ledges of oak secured with hooked iron nails

Obelix breaks in the door of No. LVII in *Asterix in Britain*. (There is no evidence that Londoners used house numbers until the 18th century)

A complete mortarium (mixing bowl), with a gritted interior designed to aid the mixing and grinding of herbs and other foods. This vessel was imported from north Gaul and carries the stamp of the potter who made it

On the other hand, much of the 1st-century pottery from Poultry was imported from Gaul and other parts of the Continent, reflecting a highly Romanised way of life from the outset of the settlement. Most households probably had sufficient income to purchase many of their daily staples, although individuals may also have been involved in small-scale market gardening and farming. Basic foods such as bread were produced locally, while garum (a strong-smelling fish sauce made from anchovies), wine, olives and olive oil and many other products were imported and sold at shops and stalls. Exotic imports found in later 1st-century pits and layers included pine nuts, mulberry, almond, pomegranate and lentils. Meat formed a large part of the diet, particularly cattle and, to a lesser degree, sheep and pigs, with smaller numbers of chickens, geese and ducks. Roman Londoners also ate wild game such as grey partridge, woodcock, red deer and brown hare, and fish from the Thames estuary – including ray, smelt, herring, eel, cod, plaice and mackerel. More unusual meals included curlew, grey heron and the common crane.

Roman Londoners ate a mixture of locally produced, imported and exotic foods

fennel

olives

mustard

almond

Cereals were the staple food in the Roman period, and spelt wheat the most popular grain, baked into bread, or made into porridge or gruel. Early Roman deposits excavated at Poultry also contained sloe, cherry and plum stones, blackberry, apple and wild strawberry pips, and shell fragments of hazelnut and walnut. Seeds of the herbs and spices coriander, dill and summer savory were also quite common.

Family and working life

We cannot be certain of the extent to which a truly Romanised routine was adopted by the population in a provincial town, although the take-up may have been significant in a town of Londinium's size and importance. In any case, family life and customs probably varied greatly even within Roman London, reflecting the cultural diversity of the population. Roman traditions of the family were very strong and these gave authority to the man at the head of the household. It is likely that they were observed by the upper classes in London and this will have constrained the freedom of women although those who came from wealthy families will have retained more independence. Many women probably worked outside the home. The bakeries, mills, fullers and shops at Poultry may well have had both male and female employees, and the wives of craftsmen and traders may have been responsible for running the shops, inns and restaurants. Officials and the well-to-do could certainly read and write, indicated by the numbers of writing tablets and stylii recovered from the Walbrook, and education was valued. Life was not entirely without its luxuries and some of the Roman families who lived at Poultry even had pet cats and dogs.

Several complete leaves from writing tablets were found during the excavations at Poultry. They were used by spreading wax across the surface and then using an iron stylus or pen to scratch a message. Impressions of words have survived on the soft pine or silver-fir tablets and may be decipherable

Drawing of a lead/tin (pewter) inkwell, similar to examples found at Pompeii

Over 50 iron stylii, used for writing, were found at Poultry. Some are elaborately decorated, such as one with an inlaid star design on its eraser stamped with the maker's name

Remarkably well-preserved cones from the stone pine, a native of the Mediterranean, were recovered from deposits near the Walbrook stream. One is shown here beside a modern specimen. The pine cone was a symbol of the god Atys and was used in religious rituals

A pipeclay figurine of Venus – Roman Londoners' houses would have contained small shrines to their gods

A late 1st-century Samian drinking cup, from southern Gaul

A typical day

The daily routine of life in a Roman town is only partially understood and based mostly on evidence from the Continent and towns such as Pompeii, but Londinium had similar facilities and life probably followed broadly similar patterns. The Roman Londoner's waking day may not have extended much beyond the hours between sunrise and sunset. For most, the pattern of the day would have been regimented, the passage of time measured by the sun's progress. Daytime was divided into 12 hours, meaning that an hour varied in length according to the seasons – in Londinium it would have been less than three-quarters of a modern hour in midwinter and nearly an hour and a half at midsummer.

The morning was the time for work. Private business was conducted at home and clients would be received there. Many people would then proceed to the forum to take part in the public business of the day. The less well-to-do would begin their labours at sunrise as well. Mid-afternoon and early evening were devoted to baths (when the water was hottest), entertainments and the daily meal.

Copper-alloy mount in the shape of a theatrical mask from comedy. Was there a theatre nearby?

Roman dice made of bone

Gaming counters made of bone

In AD 100 the residents of houses at Poultry would have made regular visits to the town's public baths at Huggin Hill (pictured), the forum at Cornhill and the amphitheatre at Guildhall Yard, all within a few minutes' walk

A beautiful 1st-century signet ring: an onyx set in a bevelled iron ring. The engraving shows the muse of comedy Thalia, holding a mask. Signet rings were used as personal stamps by their owners to emboss letters and documents

A 1st-century stud engraved with a bird, possibly an eagle

Fragment of finely made leather garment or decorative cover

Copper-alloy 'key' ring

Drawings of Roman leatherwork from Poultry: a sandal sole and part of a shoe marked with the letters FLACCI (work or property of Flacus)

An enamelled headstud brooch, typical of 2nd-century costume jewellery – robust and gaudy and worn by both sexes

The kind of clothing worn on the daily rounds was particularly important to a Roman as a person's status and age were indicated by their dress. A plain toga of natural wool was a kind of uniform to the Roman citizen. Although clothing did not survive at Poultry, over 150 Roman shoes did, and these included nailed shoes and army boots (*caliga*) and decorated sandals for indoor wear.

Roman sandal with shaped toes

Copper-alloy spoons

Venus figurine with staring eyes and hair in curls

A selection of hairpins made of bone

5

From civilised capital to abandoned ruin

AD 125 to the 5th century

The changing character of the Roman town

The excavation at Poultry has given us our best ever evidence of the character of the late Roman town, which differed substantially from the boomtown of the 1st century. The town suffered a serious setback in about AD 125, when it was completely destroyed by a fire which tore through the densely packed timber buildings (known as the Hadrianic fire after the Emperor Hadrian, who visited Britain at about this time). Roman towns throughout the Empire experienced some economic contraction in the mid 2nd century due to general economic problems, and given the disaster that London had experienced it is hardly surprising that it was slow to recover.

Bones of a red kite (lower right), common throughout England until the 18th century, were found in a layer dating from the late Roman period

A well-preserved spade, complete with an iron cutting edge, found in a roadside drain

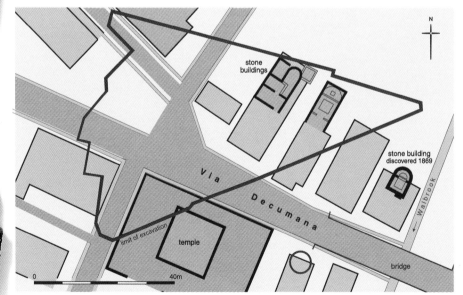

The layout of streets and buildings at Poultry at the end of the 3rd century shows that the town has changed to a mixture of timber buildings, stone buildings and rear additions, gardens and wasteland

London's grip on Britain's economy was loosened as the countryside became more self-sufficient and fewer goods were imported from the Continent. Mediterranean fruits from late Roman samples are far less common than in earlier periods, suggesting that the inhabitants now depended on locally grown crops. The movement of military personnel and goods also declined as the frontiers stabilised and campaigning declined, while parts of the administration became more devolved.

Despite the 2nd-century economic slowdown, the recent excavations have shown that new timber buildings were constructed on a larger proportion of the roadside properties at Poultry after the Hadrianic fire than seen on other London sites. The evidence also shows that the earlier property boundaries were retained all the way through to the late Roman period. The road pattern which had been established in the late 1st century continued, road surfaces kept in good repair, and roadside drains widened and deepened – possibly to incorporate the drainage of minor Walbrook tributaries.

Reconstruction view of the late Roman town at Poultry in about AD 300, looking north-west across the Walbrook stream, which is now reduced to a small channel. Many of the old timber buildings have continued in use but there are also new stone buildings and back additions, many with upper floors. The walled area to the south-east of the junction may have contained a temple. Meanwhile other properties are abandoned and become gardens or wasteland as the population declines and the economy changes

New buildings in stone

At the end of the 2nd century several of the timber buildings along the north side of the main road were extended, with new stone additions built at their backs – a development which has not been recorded on any other London archaeological site. The improvements to the roadside buildings took place at a time when London, at least in terms of expenditure on large projects, seemed to be staging something of a revival, and an impressive defensive wall was built around it.

The sophisticated stone building at the rear of the property just north-east of the road junction began life as a domestic residence. Timber piles beneath its north wall came from trees cut down between AD 223–55. The building contained five room areas and was rebuilt on two occasions, perhaps becoming a private or commercial bath. The north-east room was modified by the addition of a north apse and new mosaic floor. The north-western room was converted to a bathing chamber by removing the original floor and installing a hypocaust system, a raised tessellated floor and a hot plunge bath in one corner, probably after AD 299. The southern rooms of the building remained unheated but another heated room was added to the east in the 4th century. It is very rare to find surviving furniture from Roman Britain and this building contained one of the most important finds from the site – part of a circular, three-legged shale table.

A large post-and-plank drain along the north side of the main road and dated by dendrochronology to between AD 244 and AD 288

Part of the hypocaust (underfloor heating) system uncovered in the north-west room of the bath building. The tile stacks (*pilae*) in the foreground originally supported a raised floor above the hypocaust

Part of a mosaic floor within the apsidal room of the possible late Roman bath building

To the east of the bath building successive timber buildings were constructed from the mid 2nd century onwards. The latest of these timber buildings was built in the late 3rd century and included plank floors and a large, stone-built addition to the north as a reception room or hall. This room was unheated and contained a tessellated floor with at least two mosaic panels. The centre-panel was a complex geometric design radiating from an octagonal centre. In the northern part of the building a smaller rectangular mosaic had a figurative design. The northern side of the tessellated border, although linear, had originally been laid to a semicircular edge, suggesting that the primary phase of the room had been apsidal. Although the internal area of the room was divided by one or possibly two insubstantial partitions, these may also have been later modifications.

The owners of the building had gone to a great deal of trouble to build strong foundations, suggesting that they were aware of subsidence problems. The foundations and walls may in fact have been a 4th-century replacement of an earlier phase of the building, constructed around the precious mosaic floor which the owner was presumably determined to preserve. The superstructure of the chalk-founded building was probably timber-framed, but the juxtaposition of timber and stone building forms, even at foundation level, is extremely unusual for Roman London.

Detail of the north-west corner of the 3rd-century house which contained the geometric mosaic. Part of the tessellated floor was laid in a curving pattern even though the room was square, indicating that an earlier phase of the building was apsidal

A complex geometric patterned mosaic floor lay within a late Roman addition to the back of one of the properties, possibly a wealthy merchant's house

The stone buildings discovered in 1995 at Poultry were contemporary with another stone building just to the east, which was recorded in 1869 during the construction of Queen Victoria Street and contained a lovely mosaic known as the Bucklersbury pavement – now on display in the Museum of London. These expensive additions to properties may have been built by merchants who wanted better reception areas and living quarters behind their long-established businesses. Although less busy than in earlier centuries, late Roman London clearly retained an economic importance and status. Wealthy citizens may have maintained town houses in London and villas in the countryside. Even so, late Roman London was no tidier than the 1st-century town and some of the properties and drains were overgrown with plants such as fat hen, knotgrass, stinging nettle, goosefoot and hemlock – all plants which like rubbish dumps and manure heaps.

The Bucklersbury mosaic, from a late Roman stone building discovered during the construction of Queen Victoria Street in 1869

Recreation of a Roman Londoner's 4th-century dining room. It is possible that the chalk-built extension on one of the timber buildings at Poultry was used in this way

A tile and ragstone precinct wall was constructed at the south-east corner of the road junction in the late 2nd century, incorporating new roadside drains and forming a possible colonnade and portico around a temple

A fragment of wall plaster painted with a trompe l'oeil depiction of Corinthian columns and garlands. The plaster was found lying on a floor in the 3rd-century 'merchant's house' and may have come from a finely decorated room

Large stone buildings were also recorded on the western part of the site. A stone and tile precinct wall at the south-east corner of the Roman road junction incorporated a well-built arched culvert for the roadside drain. A second parallel stone wall lay to the south, and may be evidence of a large building located in the centre of a precinct. Most of this building lies out of reach beneath Queen Victoria Street and remains a mystery. Could it be a temple? Another late Roman stone building was found in the north-west part of the site, consisting of a load-bearing masonry wall set back from the roadside behind a corridor or portico that surrounded the building.

Mount in the form of a female panther (frequently associated with the god Bacchus) probably from an item of furniture or a cart

In the 3rd and 4th centuries well-appointed masonry buildings with underfloor heating and mosaic floors were built elsewhere in the Walbrook Valley, here at the Lothbury DLR shaft, excavated in 1988

The decline of urban life

Some of the roadside properties at Poultry became open areas or yards in the 4th century, although occupation within the stone buildings and some contemporary timber buildings continued. New floors in the bath building overlay late 4th-century pottery and coins, proving that the building was still in use. Private houses may have been the last refuge for Romanised residents at a time when many of London's public buildings, such as the forum and the amphitheatre, had disappeared.

By the late 4th century Roman Britain was in trouble. The Roman writer Marcellinus records that 'savage tribes of the Scots and Picts, who had broken the peace that had been agreed upon, were laying waste the regions near the frontiers, so that fear seized the provincials, wearied as they were by a series of past calamities'. The latest known historical reference to Londinium is to an expedition by the Emperor Theodosius in AD 367–9 to restore order in Britain after barbarian raids. Belief in the invincibility of the Roman army was badly shaken with their AD 378 defeat by the Goths in the eastern part of the Empire, although London's defensive walls continued to be maintained against the threat of Saxon raiders after this date.

A necked bowl with stamped decoration from kilns in the Oxfordshire region, dated AD 340–400+

Copper-alloy figure of Bacchus, the god of wine, holding baskets overflowing with grapes

Roman London in the late 4th century, looking north-west. The town is now encircled by defences but many of its public buildings have gone and the population is in decline

Evidence of London's final decline around the end of the 4th century may be represented by the fact that mosaic panels from the stone buildings at Poultry had been neatly excised. In one case a mosaic was replaced by a rudimentary floor of roofing tile. We may speculate that the mosaics were salvaged for their value or perhaps even removed whole by residents abandoning their homes. It is also possible that they carried pagan images and were destroyed by Christians. In any case the last residents of these buildings apparently could not afford to repair the floors or didn't feel it was worth the bother.

The collapse of Roman rule and withdrawal of troops from Britain in the early 5th century meant not only that Britain was left at the mercy of barbarian attack, but also that the political and economic basis for urban life quickly dissolved. Maintenance of the last roadside drains ended and they became clogged with silt. The roads also fell out of use, although they and the more substantial ruins clearly remained visible for some time. Londinium disappeared within a few years – the population presumably dispersing to the countryside. Some mysteries remain. The relative lack of rubble covering the late Roman buildings suggests that they were deliberately demolished and cleared, but by whom and why remains unknown. Alternatively the surface may have been scavenged clean of all usable building material by people who lived nearby.

Broken roofing tiles used to form a crude late 4th-century repair of a tessellated pavement, suggesting that the occupants had fallen on hard times

The ruins of Londinium were slowly broken down by the weather, vegetation and other natural processes. The Walbrook stream, restricted to a culvert in the late Roman period, reasserted itself. The evidence from Poultry indicates that the area was abandoned for many centuries, with no significant reoccupation until the 9th century.

An artist's impression of what the site of the Roman town may have looked like after a short period of abandonment. Nature is quickly making inroads and speeding the process of decay, while the Walbrook stream is beginning to reassert itself

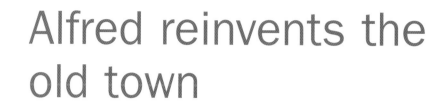

6

Alfred reinvents the old town

9th and 10th centuries

Dark Age London, the Vikings and the English

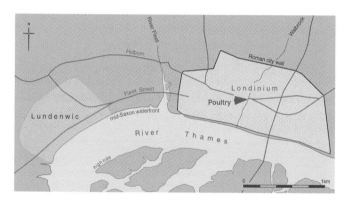

After the collapse of the Roman Empire, London is next mentioned with the founding of St Paul's in 604. The western part of the former Roman town was apparently reserved for the church and perhaps a palace. The Anglo-Saxons referred to Roman remains at London and other abandoned towns as 'the work of giants'. But despite the reference to St Paul's, archaeologists have found little or no evidence of Early and Middle Saxon occupation in the City, and even began to doubt Bede (AD 673–735), the famous historian and scholar, who referred to 'Lundenwic' as 'the market of many peoples coming by land and sea'. It was only recently discovered that Saxon London – Lundenwic – lay to the west of the City, along the Strand, an area better suited to the development of a trading-shore than the dangerous, decaying waterfronts of the old town.

Late Saxon bone comb with decorated antler connecting plates

The growth of a new settlement on the site of Londinium did not begin until the 9th century, and it was in reaction to Viking attacks on the more vulnerable settlement of Lundenwic, where there was 'a great slaughter' in 842 and again in 851. In 871 Lundenwic was occupied and the population driven out. King Alfred the Great (871–99) slowly gained the upper hand against the Danes and was able to refound the city in AD 886 – what we might today call the redevelopment of a brown-field site. The new town which was established in the embrace of the Roman defensive walls grew quickly. By the end of the 10th century London was once again the largest town in England, and attracting renewed Viking raids. It fell to the Danish king Cnut in 1016, but this had no effect on London's continued growth.

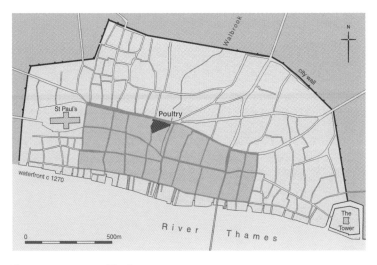

The Late Saxon town with what may have been the initial settlement in about AD 900 shown in tone

Another new start

From about the end of the 9th century London is increasingly referred to in documents as a *burh* (a fortified place or defended town) and may have developed a planned grid of streets, with north–south lanes connecting Cheapside with the Thames waterfront. At Poultry the Walbrook stream was bridged just to the north of the old Roman crossing, drainage was improved and a new east–west route established across the city. A market area developed at the eastern end of Cheapside from the late 9th century, occupying the area south of Poultry. Archaeologists discovered gravel and cobble surfaces of this date to the south of the Poultry frontage, above the Roman street junction and to the east of the church of St Benet Sherehog, where in later phases the open area appeared to have been fenced off. Large amounts of animal bone had been thrown on to the area, which also served as a rubbish tip.

Spindlewhorls used in home-based industries such as spinning were relatively rare at Poultry

Artist's reconstruction looking north-east across the Middle Saxon settlement of Lundenwic, where boats could be pulled up on a sloping riverbank – the ruins of the old Roman city are just visible in the distance (upper right of picture)

The layout of streets and buildings at Poultry in the 11th century. London fell to Cnut in 1016 and William the Conqueror in 1066 but the impact of these events had no obvious effect on contemporary buildings and properties at Poultry

Five Late Saxon sunken-floored buildings (also known as *Grubenhäuser* – pit houses, that is, timber buildings constructed in the German tradition around a manmade hollow) were recorded on the site. They would have formed simple homes and shelters, three of them near the route of Poultry and one constructed against the west wall of the ruins of a late Roman stone building. The walls and partitions of the sunken buildings

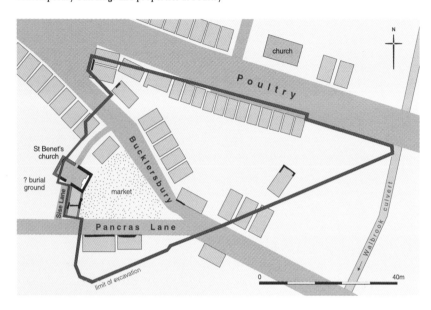

were constructed in a variety of methods, including upright earthfast posts, horizontal planking and wattle hurdles, with internal floors of brickearth, brushwood or planking. Thick organic deposits in external areas adjacent to the buildings were associated with stock enclosures, and the amount of juvenile pig bone found indicates that young pigs were being reared here.

The topography of the abandoned Roman city exerted a considerable influence over the new town. The main east–west Roman road across the city may still have been visible in the 10th century when a drainage or boundary ditch was established along its crest. At Poultry, 72 Cheapside and 36 King Street, sunken buildings were located on or close to Roman roads, suggesting that the gravelly road surface made a good base for a house.

One of the Late Saxon sunken-floored buildings had been built against the west wall of an abandoned late Roman stone building (upper right), providing the occupants with a more substantial home than most at the time

A Late Saxon drain or boundary marker cut into the crest of the abandoned east–west Roman road

Early medieval life in London

The scatter of sunken floored buildings was replaced in the late 10th century by rows of narrow timber buildings along the south side of Poultry. The Cheapside frontage was probably already built-up by this time, and the 11th-century development of Poultry and Bucklersbury reflects a growing need for trading space close to the market. The new buildings contained successive floor surfaces and may have served as shops. By the second half of the 11th century these individual structures had been replaced by a terrace of buildings divided into separate workshops by flimsy partition walls. Most of the excavated buildings contained thin brickearth, mortar or compact earth floors. Wooden planking, hay, rushes or other organic material may originally have covered these floors. The majority of the buildings were constructed of frames made with posts set directly into the ground or into timber beams laid in slots. Hearths and open fireplaces within the buildings were revealed by scorched areas of floor, tile structures and brickearth bases contained within timber surrounds. Timber buildings with wider frontages were also constructed on the north and south sides of Bucklersbury by the late 10th century.

Uncovering the extensive surfaces of what may have been a market space south of Poultry in the area which later became the junction of Bucklersbury and Pancras Lane

Reconstruction view looking west at the area of Poultry in about 1100. Several churches, including St Benet (upper left), have been established and the area has become densely occupied by small residences and shops

Ironworking waste recovered from pits and deposits in the buildings along Poultry and Bucklersbury showed that metalworking was well established by the 11th century. Other crafts and industries were represented by boneworking waste, in the form of sawn red deer antler, and small home-based activities such as spinning and weaving. Goat horncores were used in the manufacture of small objects such as gaming pieces, handles, combs and cutlery.

A small, shallow-cellared, Late Saxon building near the Walbrook crossing at the east end of Poultry. A beaten brickearth floor is enclosed by post and wattle walls to the west and north

A timber-lined hearth within a building along Bucklersbury. Evidence of ironworking (hammerscale) was found with the hearth, which was dated to 1080–1120

A Late Saxon knife with brass and copper inlay on each face. Handle missing

A group of superbly crafted shoes and ankle-boots found in 10th-century cesspits predating the church of St Benet Sherehog. The shoes are in a number of styles, some with decorative stitching and embroidery

Leather craftsman at work, based on an illustration in the 15th-century 'Mendel Housebook' from Nuremberg

To the rear of these timber buildings undeveloped space was parcelled up into individual yards in the 12th century, perhaps divided by fences. Separate backyards may be identifiable from studying the distribution and alignment of the many rubbish and cesspits which were excavated. 'Assize of Nuisance' records dating from the 14th century suggest that cesspits were often sited close to fence lines, and this may have been the case in earlier centuries as well. A similar pattern of street frontage buildings with pitted open areas to the rear has been identified at Flaxengate, Lincoln and at Coppergate, York.

These yards were home to a variety of creatures. Part of the skeleton of a grass snake and various frogs and toads were recovered from the medieval cesspits. Disused wells and cesspits often acted as accidental 'pit-fall' traps for amphibians, reptiles and small mammals. Two bones of a sparrowhawk were recovered from a 12th-century pit in the backyard of one building fronting on to Bucklersbury. Sparrowhawks were trained and used for hunting during the medieval period, and were particularly suitable for catching small birds such as quail and thrushes.

Drawing of a Late Saxon bone trial piece or motif showing a knotted animal. Seventeen animal bone trial pieces were found at Poultry, with small, interlaced, geometric designs. They may represent the result of someone practising intricate patterns or simply be playthings

The skulls of four-horned Jacob- or Hebridean-type sheep were found in several 11th-century deposits. The 'Jacob-type' breed of sheep is said to have been introduced into Britain by the Vikings

Animal bell found trodden into the surface of Bucklersbury

A Late Saxon well located in an external area between Bucklersbury and Poultry. It was constructed from part of a single oak tree trunk which had been split, hollowed out and then rejoined with timber pegs

One Late Saxon occupation deposit produced a fragment of bone from a small whale species, possibly from a local catch or a beached specimen. Chance catches and strandings would have provided bones and teeth for use as industrial raw materials, together with blubber, oil and meat. Some 12th-century deposits contained butchered horse bone scarred by sharp transverse knife-cuts associated with the use of horseflesh – probably for animal food as there is little evidence for human consumption of horseflesh in Britain after the Roman period.

7 A small parish church called St Benet

An intriguing church with an odd name

The tiny church of St Benet Sherehog was constructed in the 11th century and continued in use for six centuries until its destruction in the Great Fire. It was rediscovered in 1994, a remarkable survival sealed beneath a later burial ground. The location of St Benet is particularly interesting, as it was well away from contemporary streets and overlay the old Roman road, whose alignment it shared. The initial status of the church is mysterious, and its distance from Cheapside suggests that it was founded as a chapel in a private house and only developed a public function later.

The earliest documentary references to the church are from between 1111 and 1131, although an earlier document suggests that both St Benet and a nearby church named St Pancras were present by 1100. According to the historian John Stow (1525–1605), the name St Benet Sherehog comes from Benedict Shorne, a stockfishmonger during the reign of Edward II (1307–27), who seems to have been a new builder, repairer or benefactor of the church, the name being corrupted to Shrog or Shorehog. The church was also sometimes known as St Sithes or St Sythes. A more entertaining theory about the name was put forward by a Mr H T Riley in 1868, who suggested that it was derived from 'hogs wallowing in the shores or ditches in the vicinity which discharged themselves into the Walbrook'. Alternatively the name might have some connection with the wool trade, as a shere hog is a ram castrated after its first shearing.

The primary altar area of the church. The shallow beam slot in the foreground may be evidence of a railing, and stakeholes may be associated with church furniture

Beam slots and postholes marking the locations of the walls of the 11th-century building, located along the south side of the church and associated with metalworking and smithing

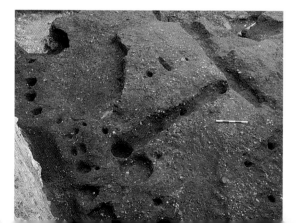

The 1994 rediscovery of the church

The 1994 excavations established that the primary phase of St Benet was a simple, single-cell rectangular building no larger than a small cottage. The limestone blocks which formed the stonework at the corners of the church were in an Anglo-Saxon style of rough long-and-short work (stones laid in an alternating vertical and horizontal pattern). Centrally positioned north and south doors show that the church could have been approached from either Cheapside to the north or Sise Lane to the south. The primary phase of the church was built almost entirely of reused Roman building material – mainly roughly squared ragstone with tile coursing – and there was no suggestion of a tower. The church contained a simple altar at its eastern end and a series of plain mortar floors. Dating evidence suggests that St Benet was built in about 1050. A fragment of a 10th-century coffin made of stone from the Barnack quarries in Lincolnshire was found incorporated into a primary wall of the church. It is possible that St Benet was built on the eastern half of an existing burial ground associated with St Pancras.

Evidence that silver was taking place in the building south of St Benet is provided by a chunk of lead-alloy waste (known as a 'litharge cake') had collected in the base of a hearth during processing

A contemporary gravel yard to the south and east of the church was overlaid by a sequence of timber buildings containing mortar floors and hearths. An 11th-century timber building standing against the south side of the church and along the east side of Sise Lane housed hearths used in metalworking, and included crucible fragments which contained traces of metal alloys. Documentary evidence from the 12th century suggests a connection between the church and a concession to trade in precious metals such as silver.

The primary phase of the 11th-century church of St Benet Sherehog, whose walls survived to a height of nearly 2 metres in places

Use and rebuilding of St Benet

A series of new mortar floors had raised the level of the church by over a metre by the 13th century. This sequence was associated with a series of altar rebuilds and a beam slot for a timber screen or railing for a small chancel in the eastern end of the church. Timber furnishings within the church were represented by postholes and slots. No burials were found with the primary phase of St Benet although some tombstones were recovered.

A later phase of the altar area

Unfortunately for St Benet and its patrons, the north and south walls of the church had been constructed directly above the soft backfills of old drains along the Roman road. As a result the church subsided and 'broke its back' within a few years, and required extensive rebuilding. A large vertical crack down through the centre of the east wall of the church is testimony to the builder's difficulties.

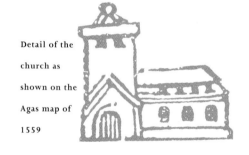

Detail of the church as shown on the Agas map of 1559

The church was the subject of further rebuilding in the later medieval period. The original building was pulled down, perhaps because of the structural damage it had suffered, and was replaced by a larger church on a slightly different alignment. Fortunately the foundations of the original church were preserved beneath the new church. At least one further rebuild took place when the second church was replaced by an even larger building aligned east–west. The later stages of the church only survived as rubble foundations and pier bases. Alterations included the addition of a separate or larger chancel to the east, an aisle to the north, and an aisle or side chapels to the south which replaced the earlier timber building there. A chapel dedicated to St Mary is recorded in 1348 and another to St Sithe in 1397.

Piers and foundations associated with later medieval phases of the church – damaged by later grave-digging

Distortion of the north wall of the church was caused by subsidence into soft underlying deposits

Documents refer to a number of burials within the body of the later church. Some of these burials were excavated in 1994 but the majority had already been removed by the graves of the post-Great Fire cemetery. Tombstones, some with inlaid brass lettering in a Lombardic script, were found and can be related to the 13th-century church. Documentary evidence includes the instructions left in the will of John Fressh, mercer and mayor, buried at St Benet in 1397, and particularly evocative of life and death at the time:

> For one year after my death one penny for ale and bread to be paid every Friday to each prisoner in Newgate; 100 marks to discharge as many prisoners as possible with debts of less than five marks; 1000 masses to be said per week for 10 weeks after death for my soul; 100 marks for funeral expenses. And I will that my executors shall arrange for four and twenty large candles and a seemly light of wax about my corpse, and that folk should don a black cloth, which it is seemly should be worn, and that they make communion; and also that they give to each torch-bearer on the day of my obsequies a coat with a hood of black.

A Purbeck marble grave headstone recovered from St Benet and dating from the 12th/13th century. The inscription says 'Here lies in the tomb Alice the wife of Peter'. A complex cross is carved on the reverse

Later events at St Benet reflected general discontent with the Roman Catholic Church, and William Sawtre, a curate of the church, was one of the first heretics to be burned at Smithfield for Lollardy under an Act of Parliament in 1401. Very little of the late church survived due to the insertion of burials in the 17th and 18th centuries, although a few glazed and decorated late 15th-century floor tiles were recovered. The church was repaired and beautified in 1628 at the cost of parishioners, 'being very much decayed and perished' according to Strype's updated edition of Stow.

View east along Pancras Lane in 1851 with the burial ground of St Benet in the left foreground – the only clue that a church stood on the site up until the Great Fire

8 The burgeoning medieval City

12th to 15th centuries

An energetic town

By the end of the 12th century London had outdistanced other English towns in both population and wealth. Increasing demand for space led to buildings encroaching on to streets and other open spaces, as well as the subdivision of existing building plots. At the same time a network of minor streets and lanes evolved behind the main streets. Pancras Lane was a new street in the 13th century, and small shops or stalls were soon built along its south side.

Metalworkers, in particular smiths and ironmongers, continued to be well represented in the rows of shops and workshops along Poultry and Bucklersbury. In 1300 the west end of Poultry was known as Ironmongers Row and served visitors to the great Cheapside market. The eastern half of the street was called 'La Lorimerie' or Lorimers' Row, as its shops made and sold metal bridle pieces ('lorimer' is a Middle English word for a maker of small iron objects and comes from the Latin word *lorum*, meaning 'strap' or 'thong'). Other specialised manufacturing, such as the production and sale of knives and spurs, was located near the eastern end of Cheapside. One of the buildings excavated at Poultry was identified as the dwelling of Reginald le Hauberger, a leading armourer.

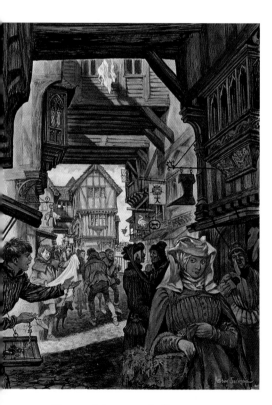

The crowded streets and tall, overhanging houses of medieval London, as depicted by artist Peter Jackson

A very rare early medieval musical instrument – an end-blown horn with fingerholes – may be a precursor of the cornet. No sign of any decoration or a mouthpiece survived. An 11th-century French Book of Psalms contains an illustration of a similar horn

Increasing wealth

By the middle of the 13th century large stone houses had been constructed away from the major streets. The character of the area changed as higher land values forced manufacturing to move to less central sites. With the establishment of the Stocks Market near present-day Mansion House, poulterers and grocers arrived in the area. More lucrative activities also sprang up, including trade in imported luxuries, and money lending became more prominent. At Bucklersbury wealthy merchants and financiers could be close to the Cheapside market where much of their business was carried out, but away from the hustle and bustle of the main commercial streets.

Part of a chalk-lined pit associated with the property of the Tolesan family

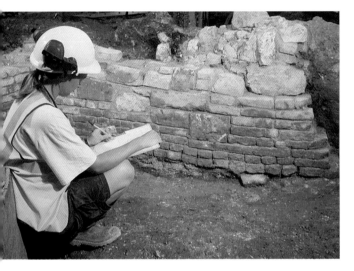

The layout of chalk rubble foundations, stone-lined wells and cesspits along the south side of Poultry have helped archaeologists to reconstruct the ground plans of several large masonry buildings, and it is possible to follow the histories of many of these residences. One 13th-century property was owned by the powerful and wealthy Tolesan family, merchants who migrated to London from Toulouse. Timber buildings were generally replaced by new stone-built shops attached to the larger houses at the rear, and the front of the Tolesan property was divided into two shops, one occupied by a lorimer.

A medieval counting table. The Bucklersbury property of the Riccardi merchants of Lucca became the first financial house in the City in the 13th century

Another large property, on the north side of Bucklersbury, was occupied by John Mansel, who was Henry III's clerk and one of his leading counsellors in the mid 13th century. Evidence of London's rise as an important financial centre is represented by this property, which became the headquarters of merchants of the Society of the Riccardi of Lucca shortly after Mansel died in 1265. These merchants sold spices and textiles and were also granted permission to run a money exchange at the property – making it the City's very first financial trading house – while the street outside became a regular meeting place for people wanting to exchange financial information.

In 1301 the property became the residence of William Servat, a dealer in wine, cloth and spices who had close contacts with Italian merchants. Servat built a large gatehouse tower, whose chalk rubble foundations were found on the site. In about 1317 the buildings were given to Edward II's consort Queen Isabel, who used the property as her financial base in the City, but in 1355 it was once again let out to merchants of Lucca. Bucklersbury continued to be a centre for financial dealings until this trade shifted eastwards to Lombard Street sometime shortly after 1367.

A much later incident involving Servat's Tower was recorded by Stow and shows that demolition work has always been dangerous:

> This tower of late years was taken down by one Buckle, a grocer, meaning in place thereof to have set up and built a goodly frame of timber; but the said Buckle greedily labouring to pull down the old tower, a part thereof fell upon him, which so sore bruised him that his life was thereby shortened, and another that married his widow set up the new prepared frame of timber, and finished the work.

The development and function of properties at the end of the 13th century can be identified from documentary evidence and compared with the archaeological findings

Another great stone building lay to the south of Bucklersbury. It was called The Barge – perhaps because barges could be dragged up the Walbrook stream that far – and was owned by the Bukerel family, the street deriving its name from them. By the 16th century the house had been divided into tenements and one of the occupants was Thomas More, who on several occasions was visited by Erasmus there.

Braun & Hogenburg's map of London, 1572. London's expansion demanded a more reliable water supply than either wells or conduits could provide

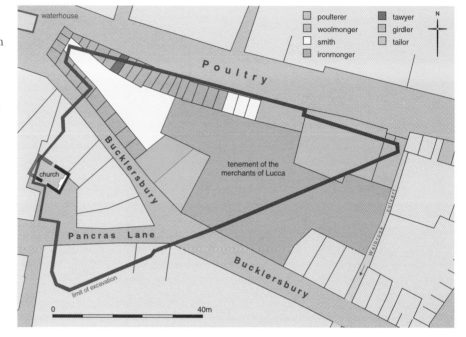

Discovery of the Great Conduit

In the summer of 1994 archaeologists watching sewer diversion work at the junction of the medieval streets of Cheapside and Bucklersbury discovered a perfectly preserved underground chamber. The arched interior had a greensand stone-flag floor and an ornate doorway at its east end which led to a stairway up to the medieval street surface.

A late medieval copper-alloy clasp

The chamber was part of an ambitious 13th-century system which carried water to the City via lead pipes and cisterns, all the way from the Tyburn stream 3 kilometres to the west (near the junction of present-day Oxford Street and Marylebone Lane). London's rapid growth had led to a demand for clean water which could not be met by individual wells. Construction of the conduit between 1236–45 was a considerable achievement, funded by wealthy citizens and City officials, although the gravity flow and constant leaks meant that the supply was sometimes meagre. The chamber discovered in 1994 was part of the final Conduit House or cistern along the route of what was known as the 'Great Conduit', rebuilt in 1286 'with stone castellations'.

Excavating a medieval well between Bucklersbury and Pancras Lane

The route of the 13th-century City water supply from the Tyburn to the Great Conduit. The supply was extended westwards to Paddington Fields in the 15th century

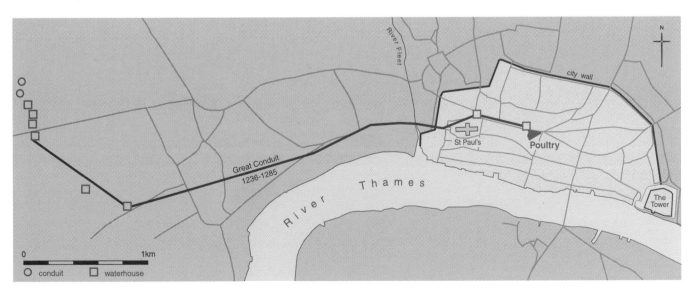

River Fleet

city wall

St Paul's

Poultry

River Thames

Great Conduit 1236-1285

The Tower

N

0   1km

O conduit   □ waterhouse

The history of the Great Conduit gives us a glimpse into the social history of medieval London. The water was free to all, but arguments arose about illegal private tapping and overuse by trades such as brewers. At the coronation of Edward I in August 1274 the Cheapside conduit allegedly flowed with red and white wine. As London grew, new sources and conduits were developed and the Great Conduit was enlarged in 1479. By the late 16th century even the conduit supplies were inadequate, so private water companies and pumped supplies were established. After the Great Fire the New River Company and others extended their distribution systems and the Great Conduit was not rebuilt. The Great Conduit cistern has been preserved beneath the modern street at the east end of Cheapside.

The Agas 'copperplate map' of 1559 showing the area around Poultry, with St Benet Sherehog and the Great Conduit clearly identifiable

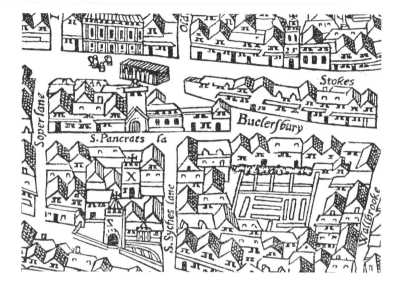

The underground cistern of the Great Conduit, constructed in the 13th century and preserved beneath the junction of Cheapside and Poultry

62

Food on the table: the diet of 12th- and 13th-century London

Over 42,000 animal bones were collected from Late Saxon and medieval layers at Poultry, while other food waste was recovered from soil samples. This material tells us a great deal about medieval Londoners' diet. As in the Roman layers, charred cereal grains were found, but bread wheat had replaced spelt, rye was more common than in Roman times and oats were much more abundant. Lentils, peas and horsebeans (similar to modern broad beans) were also found. The range of fruit was similar to that from the late Roman period, including a few grapes and figs, but there was a greater reliance on locally grown produce such as sloes, plums, cherries, apples, blackberries and hazelnuts. A single peach stone probably came from a wealthy household; peach trees are known to have been grown in the royal garden at Westminster during the 13th century. Occasional flax and hemp seeds were also found: these crops were probably being grown for their stem fibres, which were used to make textiles and rope.

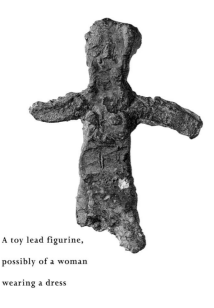

A toy lead figurine, possibly of a woman wearing a dress

Medieval Londoners made greater use of fish than their Roman predecessors: freshwater species were found as well as fish from the Thames estuary and nearby coasts. Londoners were particularly fond of eels but also ate salmon, sprat and flounder, and more expensive catches such as sole, turbot and haddock. One rare item found was a sturgeon, which came from a 12th-century deposit. The meat diet was still based on beef, with some pork, but the medieval Londoner ate more mutton, chicken, goose and deer. The great variety of foods available to Londoners – not just to the wealthy merchants but also to unskilled workers on the economic margins – reflects the success of the medieval city. London's population may have been greater at the end of the 13th century, before the onrush of the Black Death, than it would be again for nearly 200 years.

Roebuck skull and antler. Sawn-off red deer antler tines were found in some quantity and may indicate that boneworking took place nearby

Bone skates were usually made from the long bones of horses or cattle. They were then attached to the shoe with thongs

9

'This glorious and ancient city'

16th to 18th centuries

An ever expanding metropolis

Tin-glazed 'delftware' tiles showing biblical scenes are Dutch imports dating from the 17th century. Scenes depicted include Jonah being disgorged by the whale

John Stow, who wrote his *Survey of London* in 1598, saw the birth of the modern capital during his lifetime. Born in 1525, as a boy he would have known a compact London of fewer than 100,000 souls and with the countryside within view. By 1600 the population had more than doubled and by 1650 it had doubled again. Despite the setbacks caused by plague and fire, at the end of the 17th century London was the largest city in Europe. Stow's London was a magnet to people from all over the British Isles and the Continent, much as it is today.

London in the 17th century was an overcrowded, unwholesome and dangerous place. Severe outbreaks of the bubonic plague in 1603, 1625 and 1636 caused the City to introduce a series of measures to deal with overcrowding and poor sanitation. These changes were clearly ineffective. The diarist John Evelyn – who was also a commissioner for improving the streets and buildings of London – said in an address to Parliament in 1661: 'that this glorious and ancient City ... should wrap her stately head in clouds of smoke and sulphur, so full of stink and darkness, I deplore with just indignation'. Evelyn decried the 'congestion of misshapen and extravagant houses' and streets which were 'so narrow and incommodious', and went on to suggest that sweet-smelling trees should be planted to purify the air.

Scattered cellars, wells and pits dating from before the Great Fire were recorded during the dig. One pit contained an assemblage of very fine glass vessels and imported goods that may have belonged to a well-to-do family. Research shows that the rich and poor lived in close proximity, although the wealthy tended to occupy more spacious buildings set back from the street frontages. Shops opened directly on to Poultry and the poorest residents lived in small rooms in the upper storeys.

An assemblage of 17th-century Westerwald and Frechen stoneware imported from the Rhineland included fine tablewares such as tankards and elaborate jugs decorated with 'peacock eyes' and 'lion-masks'

London viewed from Southwark in about 1650, before its destruction in the Great Fire

The contents of another pit included the skull of a very young calf which may be waste from the consumption of veal, as well as small birds such as thrushes, finches and larks which are no longer legally caught or consumed in the British Isles. The same deposit contained the remains of an adult rat, probably the black rat (*Rattus rattus*), an intermediate host of the plague. A contemporary well contained at least 15 black rats and three mice.

The unruliness of 17th-century London was recorded by the diarist Samuel Pepys. On 30 September 1661 he witnessed an extraordinary brawl between the French and Spanish ambassadors and their staff, who were determined to gain the prime spot next to the king's coach during a procession. Having made it along Poultry, 'in Cheapside the Spaniard hath got the best of it and killed three of the French coach-horses and several men and is gone through the City next to our King's coach. At which it is strange to see how all the City did rejoice. And endeed, we do naturally all love the Spanish and hate the French.'

The poet Katherine Philips (1631–64), known as the Matchless Orinda, was the daughter of a Bucklersbury merchant. She died of smallpox and was buried at St Benet Sherehog near to her baby son, Hector, who had died on 2 May 1655, and whose epitaph she had composed:

> What on Earth deserves our trust?
> Youth and Beauty both are dust.
> Long we gathering are with pain,
> What one moment calls again.
> Seven years childless marriage past,
> A Son, a son is born at last:
> So exactly lim'd and fair,
> Full of good Spirits, Meen, and Air
> As a long life promised,
> Yet, in less than six weeks dead.
> Too promising, too great a mind
> In so small room to be confin'd:
> Therfore, as fit in Heav'n to dwell,
> He quickly broke the Prison shell.
> So the subtle Alchimist,
> Can't with Hermes Seal resist
> The powerful spirit's subtler flight,
> But t'will bid him long good night.
> And so the Sun if it arise
> Half so glorious as his Eyes,
> Like this Infant, takes a shrowd,
> Buried in a morning cloud.

Crime and punishment

The Poultry Compter was one of several small ward prisons in the City. It dated from the medieval period and was rebuilt after the Great Fire. In the late 17th century London could be a violent place where tavern or street brawls often led to the use of knives and swords. There are many references to scrapes with the law which resulted in a night in the Poultry Compter and Ben Jonson (d. 1637) mentions the Compter in his plays. In 1700 a group of friends thrown into the Compter for after-hours drinking were released in the morning and went directly to The Rose Tavern in Poultry where they 'laughed at our night's adventure and cursed the constable'. A more sinister use of the 17th-century Compter involved the imprisonment of black people, who were effectively treated as lost property. West Indian plantation owners often brought slaves to England as servants. Slavery was not legal in England but those who ran away or were turned out had little chance of justice and were imprisoned until 'ownership' could be established.

The Poultry Compter, one of the City's prisons

Black rat

Plague and fire

In 1665 London suffered its worst plague year. Pepys's eyewitness accounts describe some of the fears and anxieties of the time. On 7 June 1665 he passed houses of plague victims, which were shut up for 40 days with the residents inside: 'It put me into an ill conception of myself and my smell, so that I was forced to buy some roll tobacco to smell to and chaw – which took away the apprehension.' Pepys's reference to tobacco is significant as the weed was believed to offer some protection – word had it that no tobacconist died of the plague.

The plague was at its worst during August and September. With the onset of colder weather the plague declined, but it had claimed nearly 100,000 victims. People remained unaware of the connection between the plague, rats and fleas, but fortunately there were no more outbreaks of the disease in London.

Samuel Pepys. In his diaries he expressed a reluctance to wear his new wig for fear that the hair may have been taken from the heads of plague victims – he was correct to be worried, as plague-carrying fleas were a serious danger

A plague broadsheet, being 'a true Account of how many persons died Weekly ... and the Greatness of the Calamity and the Violence of the Distemper in the Last Year 1665'. The list includes St Benet and other parishes from Poultry

Parish's Names.	1625.		1636.		1665.	
	Bu.	Pl.	Bu.	Pl.	Bu.	Pl.
Albans Woodstr.	188	78	42	13	200	121
Albollows Bark.	397	283	142	32	514	330
Albollows Breadstr.	34	14	14	2	35	16
Albollows the Great	442	302	123	42	455	416
Albollows Honylane	18	8	3	0	10	5
Albollows the lesse	259	205	47	8	239	175
Albollows Lumb. str.	86	44	22	2	90	62
Albollows Stayning	183	138	28	5	185	112
Albollows the Wall	301	155	111	40	500	356
Alphage	240	150	62	11	271	115
Andrew Hubbard	146	101	26	10	71	25
Andrew Und. shaft	219	149	44	11	274	189
Andrew Wardrope	373	191	120	44	476	308
Ann Aldersgate	196	128	104	68	282	197
Ann Blackfryers	336	215	153	59	652	467
Antholins Parish	62	31	24	7	58	33
Bartholmew Parish	73	49	20	2	83	20
Barthol. Exch.			19	0	73	51
Bennet Fynk	108	57	25	7	47	22
Bennet Gr. Church	48	14	16	1	57	41
Bennet Paulswharf	216	131	112	49	355	173
Bennet Sherehog	24	8	9	0	11	
Botolph Billingsg.	99	66	30	9	83	50
Christs Church	611	371	183	70	653	467
Christophers	48	28	13	6	60	47
Clement Eastcheap	87	71	18	3	38	20
Dionis Backchurch	99	59	17	2	78	27

London was struck by another disaster the following year. The Great Fire began in Pudding Lane on Sunday, 2 September 1666 and burned for six days. Driven by a strong east wind it swept through the crowded, wooden houses at the end of a hot, dry summer. All of the buildings around Bucklersbury and Poultry were burned to the ground on the Monday, including St Benet. The use of explosives to demolish buildings and create firebreaks eventually proved effective, but most of the City had been destroyed. Very few people lost their lives as a result of the fire, but 13,200 houses had burned down, along with 87 churches.

Once again London was quickly rebuilt. Christopher Wren dreamed of an entirely new plan with wide, straight roads and, while this did not happen, new ordinances were introduced specifying that stone and brick should replace the ramshackle timber buildings. Disaster was turned to opportunity and London continued to grow ever larger and richer.

Hollar's engraving showing the effect of the Great Fire of 1666. Within the area shown white only the ruins of a few of the more substantial stone buildings and churches still stood

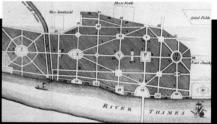

Designs for the rebuilding of London drawn up by Sir Christopher Wren (top) and John Evelyn. Both were turned down by the City fathers in 1666 as unworkable

Contemporary view of the Great Fire by an unknown Dutch artist

The burial ground at St Benet

The church of St Benet was not rebuilt after the Great Fire and the parish was amalgamated with St Stephen Walbrook. The land that St Benet had occupied was used as a subsidiary burial ground for the new parish. Up to its closure in 1853, around 220 burials took place, mostly in the 18th century and in wooden coffins decorated with nameplates, fittings and studs. The burials offer a variety of insights into the people who lived in this part of London at the time – from the very poor to the wealthy and privileged.

In 1994 the site of the burial ground was a dark and ill-maintained open space containing two trees. The top of the family vault of Michael Davison was just visible. Davison was a wealthy and respected member of the parish who died on 24 June 1676. In his will he left a property in Holloway to the parish on the condition that they 'shall for ever from time to time keepe in repair and uphold my toombe in the churchyard'.

Excavation of the post-Great Fire burial ground

With the exception of the years immediately following the Great Fire, very few wealthy people were buried at St Benet, most choosing the vault at St Stephen instead. The burial ground at St Benet became a resting-place for the poor. The parish registers record that on 22 December 1724 'a poor man who fell down in the street' was buried there, the vestry paying the bill. On 16 April 1728 'Mary, a parish child' was found in the street in the parish and was 'taken up and baptised the same night'; she was also buried the same day. Many foundlings – children found abandoned in the street – are listed in the baptism records for the parish, the names often being derived from where the child was found: hence Mary Bucklersbury, Anne Bennet, Thomas Benet, Esther Pancras, Mary Sise and Edward Buckler.

The tomb of Mayor John Maurois who died in January 1673

The archaeology of death

The skeletons excavated at St Benet include all age groups and their study has found evidence of the diseases of poverty such as tuberculosis and rickets, which are associated with overcrowding and malnutrition. Many of the children and a few adults had distorted legs, and evidence of the effects of pollution can be seen in the inflamed sinuses of some skulls. By contrast, other burials in the cemetery show a strange condition of the spine known as 'DISH', believed to be caused by a high-calorie diet and indicating that some of the older men were overweight.

Excavating one of the burials at St Benet

All the people buried at St Benet seem to have received reasonable medical attention during their lives. Broken limbs had healed well, probably because of careful setting and splinting. Dentistry was another matter, with both rich and poor having bad teeth, due to the arrival of cheap sugar.

Study of the skeletons has also turned up some surprises. In many cases the nails used to fasten down the coffin lids had pierced the limbs of those buried. Scrimping on materials had resulted in shallow coffins and the nails were hammered straight into the uncomplaining bodies of the recently dead.

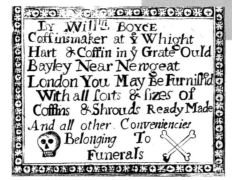

Funerals

The growing population and high death rate in late 17th-century London meant that funerals became a large and lucrative business. Cabinetmakers and other tradesmen became undertakers by producing coffins and providing other arrangements and supplies for funerals – which they advertised by way of trade cards. Elaborate funerals of the wealthy sometimes took place a couple of weeks after death, but for the poor a swift interment was the rule – especially in hot weather, as embalming was still rare and expensive. Funerals were an important reflection of the status of the deceased and the ignominy of a pauper's funeral was something to be avoided. Fancy coffins and funerals were sometimes beyond a family's means and on other occasions the undertaker may have cheated on the materials – the profession gained a bad reputation. Arrival at London's overcrowded churchyards and burial grounds presented other problems and grave diggers often disturbed burials in order to make space for new arrivals. In *Bleak House* Charles Dickens describes the lack of space for a new burial – 'They put him wery nigh the top. They was obliged to stamp upon it to git it in. I could unkiver it for you with my broom, if the gate was open. That's why they locks it, I s'pose.'

An upper arm bone from a burial penetrated by two coffin nails that have trapped part of the coffin lid and burial shroud

A macabre 17th-century undertaker's trade card

A coffin plate from one of the St Benet burials

Mad hatters

Working conditions in 18th century London were often unpleasant and unhealthy. Brick-lined sumps behind properties in Bucklersbury were found to be heavily contaminated with mercury waste. Exposure to mercury is a serious risk to health, and archaeologists working in the area had to wear full protective clothing. In 1760 there was a shop called the Hatt & Beaver at Poultry – the best hats were made of beaver, although most were a mixture of wool and rabbit fur. Hatmakers used a mixture of mercury solution and nitric acid to soften fur and wool so that it could be felted. The felt was then shaped using heat, water and manipulation, and finally put on to blocks or forms and stacked in ovens. The process released mercury fumes which attacked the nervous system of the workers who inhaled them, eventually causing serious damage visible as 'hatters' shakes'. By the end of the 18th century the medical profession was beginning to notice the deteriorating health of hatmakers, and in 1866 the term 'mad hatter' was guaranteed a place in the popular lexicon when Lewis Carroll published *Alice's Adventures in Wonderland*.

Archaeologists excavating features contaminated by mercury

The 'Mad Hatter's tea party' from *Alice's Adventures in Wonderland*. Madness was commonly associated with hatmaking due to the disastrous effects on health resulting from the use of mercury in the felting process

10 Heart of the Empire

19th century

London – centre of the world

When archaeologists began evaluation work at Poultry in 1994 the site was still occupied by Victorian buildings. They included Mappin & Webb and many other exuberant examples of elaborate Victorian Gothic, Venetian, Italianate and Renaissance styles constructed between 1869 and 1875 – the very embodiment of Victorian London.

London at the height of the British Empire was a unique and remarkable city – by far the largest and wealthiest in the world. Its rapid growth was powered by leaps in manufacturing production and trade, and brought to fruition through the speculative financing and building of mile upon mile of new housing. The commercial heart of the new metropolis was the City, which had begun to change from its earlier mixture of merchants and shopkeepers, many of whom 'lived above the shop', to become a centre for banking, insurance and counting houses.

Horwood's plan of London, 1794–9, showing the layout of the area around Poultry before construction of Queen Victoria Street

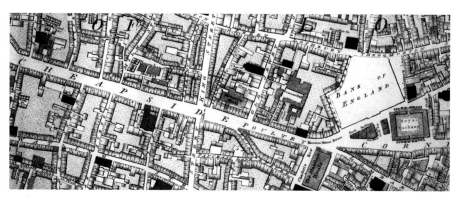

View of 1810 showing Bucklersbury with Pancras Lane on the left. The dark street and narrow housefronts show how the area retained some of its medieval character after the Great Fire

Between 1850 and 1900 the resident population of the City fell from around 130,000 to less than 30,000, the process driven not only by economic and social change but by the forced evictions of the poor which accompanied the construction of new roads, railways and office buildings. At the same time more and more people worked in the City: by 1850 over 200,000 workers walked to their jobs in the City every day.

The second half of the 19th century witnessed intense building works in the City. One of the most ambitious developments was the construction of Queen Victoria Street by the Metropolitan Board of Works, coinciding with the digging of the new underground railway to Mansion House Station. The broad new street, which was opened in sections between 1867 and 1871, was part of a much larger scheme which included construction of the Embankment, and was intended to relieve traffic congestion all the way from the City to the West End. Although some streets, such as Poultry itself, had been widened after the Great Fire, much of the City had retained its medieval character, exemplified by narrow lanes like Bucklersbury. The new road smashed through this pattern.

An 1850s' suggestion to route traffic underground – congestion had become a serious issue and the construction of Queen Victoria Street was the solution eventually chosen

A rather fanciful 1862 proposal for an elevated footbridge across Poultry at Mansion House, intended to allow safe passage for pedestrians

1870 auction particulars for the 'Mappin & Webb' building. It was as much the product of speculative development as the 1996 building which has replaced it

The Victorian buildings at Poultry

Over 500 properties had to be bought up along the proposed route of Queen Victoria Street, a process which took several years to complete, with demolition beginning in 1868. Because of the raking angle of the new street, the plots created along its sides tended to be triangular. These sites were bought up by private developers who wanted to construct larger office buildings, often with lifts and iron-girder framing, but which still obeyed the traditions and hierarchies of classical architecture. In 1851 John Ruskin had written the influential *The Stones of Venice*, in which he advocated the adoption of a Venetian Gothic style, arguing that the mercantile traditions and rich architectural heritage of Venice were an appropriate example for London to take up. As a result, the City witnessed the construction of many innovative and architecturally progressive buildings during the 1860s and 1870s.

'London improvements: demolitions in the Poultry for the new street leading from the Thames embankment', from the *Illustrated London News*, January 1869

John Belcher Junior's Mansion House Buildings at 2–10 Queen Victoria Street, illustrated by Walmsley after Benjamin Sly in *The Builder*, 1871

One of the best known of these new buildings was John Belcher Junior's Mansion House Buildings, constructed at 2–10 Queen Victoria Street in 1870 and known from its principal tenants as the Mappin & Webb building. The father and son architectural practice of John & John Belcher had recently completed 16–17 Poultry in the new Venetian style for James Wheeler, a hosier and outfitter. At Mappin & Webb the younger Belcher designed and built an outstanding example of the new Gothic style in Bath stone and granite, which drew on 12th-century French traditions in its use of arcaded and traceried openings and decorative carving. The point of the triangular site was handled effortlessly, the arcades sweeping around in an unbroken curve, with a rounded arcaded tower at the higher floors topped by a conical roof and giving the whole area a focal point.

Similar buildings were constructed to the west. At 1–2 Poultry, in 1875, John Belcher took on an even more tightly triangular plot of ground at the junction with Bucklersbury and produced a quite different style with oriel windows, pinnacles and turrets. At 4–5 Poultry the restaurateur Frederick Sawyer – having earlier acquired the Georgian building at 3 Poultry which housed an oyster house owned by James Pimm (the inventor of Pimm's) – hired R H Moore in 1870 to build a new restaurant with a facade of Gothic arcades. At 9–11 Poultry a larger block which stretched through to 24 Queen Victoria Street was developed by Major J F Wieland in 1875. Unlike his developer neighbours, Wieland was not a shopkeeper intending to let out the upper floors. Wieland employed the architect Frederick Ward to design a building of Venetian Gothic arcades decorated with carved rosettes.

Mansion House Buildings (Mappin & Webb) on a very quiet morning in 1897, with the Mansion House to the left

The original No. 1 Poultry – at the west end of
the street at its junction with Bucklersbury

Also in 1875, Frederick Chancellor designed and built a remarkable red brick and
Dumfries stone edifice at 12–13 Poultry. The building was only a single bay in width,
dominated by broad windows. Terracotta panels by the French sculptor Joseph Kremer
were situated between the floors and depicted the processions of four monarchs
through the City. From the top these were Edward VI (1547), Queen Elizabeth (1558),
Charles II (1660) and Queen Victoria (1844). The panels have been restored and can
now be seen on the north side of the new building.

To the east at 14–15 Poultry an Italianate building designed by A Bridgman had been
constructed in 1872. Nos 16–17 Poultry was occupied by a building constructed in
Venetian style in 1868 by John Belcher Senior. Victorian buildings were replaced by
later Edwardian buildings at 6 Poultry and 7–9 Poultry (Revenue House) and
completed the Poultry facade. Many of these buildings extended through to form the
facades on the east side of Bucklersbury, with the exception of No. 38, which was a
narrow Gothic building dating from the 1860s.

Pimm's restaurant at No. 3 Poultry,
from a 1946 photograph

Detail of lower two terracotta panels with
shopfronts below, from a post-war photograph

The western side of Bucklersbury included a bodega – a Victorian wine bar – built in 1874 at Nos 5–6. To its south at 7–9 Bucklersbury were Albert Chambers, the Green Man public house and Victoria Chambers, dating from 1872 and 1877, and designed by Edmund Woodthorpe. West of the Mappin & Webb building, 12–22 Queen Victoria Street was completed in 1872 and was designed in a Renaissance style which was restrained compared with its neighbours, with arcades of rounded arches and round-headed dormer windows above the cornice. At 26–38 Queen Victoria Street, Frederick Ward designed Imperial Buildings in 1873 in a Renaissance style but with a much more emphatic result. Ornamental tiers of arcades rose to a frieze, cornice and balustrade – to create what has sometimes been referred to as a 'wedding-cake' style.

In 1877, a magazine called the *Almanac* described the new buildings at Poultry in very unflattering terms and found them to be: 'in very questionable taste, the ornaments tawdry, overcrowded, misplaced, and obtrusive, but the ensemble is not ineffective'. A century later the same buildings would be called the finest group of High Victorian commercial architecture in the City. Then, as now, anything new in a historic area tended to meet resistance, while anything old gained a patina of respectability by comparison.

Construction of Queen Victoria Street in 1869 (foreground) cut through the medieval street pattern of the City, creating awkward triangular sites

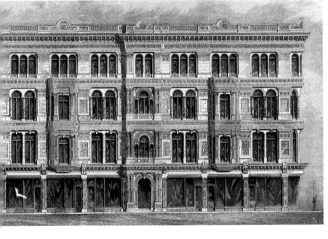

Frederick Ward's Imperial Buildings at 26–38 Queen Victoria Street was an exuberant construction in Italian Renaissance style, reproduced here from *The Builder*, 1874. It noted that the building required particularly deep foundations as 'treacherous ground in the bed of the old Walbrook' crossed the site

Goad Insurance map of 1886, showing the area around Poultry and naming the many small businesses present

11 A new building that might just be a masterpiece

The battle for planning permission

The new building at 1 Poultry, designed by the late Sir James Stirling, was completed nearly 40 years after the idea of a City landmark for the site was first conceived. Sixteen Victorian buildings were demolished to make way for the Stirling building and eight of these were listed Grade II – buildings considered to be of special historic or architectural importance either individually or as a group. Nearly everyone was opposed to their demolition.

Mappin & Webb, with the Mansion House on the left

The now familiar scene in the 1930s – Mappin & Webb and traffic at the junction at Queen Victoria Street and Poultry

But were Mappin & Webb and the other buildings demolished at Poultry important parts of our architectural heritage or just 'typical Victorian buildings'? With the exception of John Belcher Junior, the architects who built at Poultry were relatively unknown and remained so, a small group who concentrated on building offices in the City of London. Belcher was recognised as one of the 19th century's most original architects. Even so, compared to the love for everything Georgian, Victorian architecture, particularly Gothic Revival buildings, had few friends until relatively recently. The Stirling building may be seen as a striking landmark by one of the 20th century's greatest architects, or as just another example of a large, commercial building out of scale and sympathy with its surroundings. Our views on architecture tend to reflect personal tastes rather than the measurement of objective criteria, and it is hardly surprising that public inquiries concerning the replacement of favourite buildings can become emotionally charged.

There are approximately 360,000 statutorily listed buildings in England at present – buildings which cannot be altered inside or out without permission. Listing also includes red postboxes and telephone boxes. Building conservation is very popular – preservation of an 'old' or 'important' building is an act of reassurance, given the speed of change witnessed in many of our towns and the countryside. Saving a cherished old building can represent a victory over such disparate 'enemies' as the Blitz, poor town planners, bad architects, greedy land-owners and demanding multinationals.

The City of London was heavily bombed during the war. The ticket hall at Bank Underground Station suffered a direct hit on 11 January 1941, killing 57 people

There was no love lost between the conservationists and modern architects at Poultry and the battle lines were clearly drawn during two planning inquiries and an appeal to the House of Lords. In the first inquiry, in 1984, both the City Corporation and the GLC Planning Committee lined up against Peter Palumbo and his architects. At issue was planning permission for a new square and an 18-storey steel and glass office tower designed by the German-born architect Ludwig Mies van der Rohe. Expert witnesses who were supporters of the redevelopment attacked the Victorian buildings as 'a motley collection', while others viewed their lack of uniformity as a positive attribute representing the range of styles used in late Victorian commercial building.

The new Mansion House Square would have created excellent views of Lutyens' Midland Bank to the north of Poultry, George Dance's Mansion House to the east and Wren's St Stephen Walbrook to the south-east. However, the current was running against the Mies scheme. The appeal was dismissed by the Secretary of State in a letter of May 1985, which agreed with the inspector that although the Mies tower was of great distinction, both it and the square were unsuitable for such an historic area. Future redevelopment was not entirely ruled out in the letter, which suggested that different proposals might be acceptable. The door was left ajar.

Poster used by 'SAVE' in their campaign

A new and very different proposal was submitted in 1986 – a much smaller building designed by James Stirling and restricted to the triangular area between Poultry and Queen Victoria Street – but this was also turned down. In 1988 Palumbo's team began another appeal to the Secretary of State for the Environment, having failed to gain the necessary permissions from the City, who remained opposed to the demolition of the eight listed buildings and loss of the historic street of Bucklersbury. At the appeal the developer was faced by a battery of opponents, including English Heritage, the Corporation of London, SAVE Britain's Heritage, The Victorian Society and many others. This was also a time when Prince Charles was outspoken in his criticism of much modern architecture, including the Stirling building, which he allegedly referred to as looking like a 1930s' wireless set.

A 1984 newspaper article chronicling Palumbo's efforts to win support for the Mansion House Square scheme

There was little public sympathy for the argument that too much conservation would 'freeze the City' and prevent much needed economic growth. Of over 800 letters from the public received at the inquiry, only 29 supported the redevelopment, although Mappin & Webb – tenants of 2–10 Queen Victoria Street since 1872 – described their cramped premises as 'totally unsuitable to modern retailing'.

At the end of the second inquiry in June 1988, the inspector concluded that the Victorian buildings, although of merit, were not that special. On the other hand the Stirling building 'would be a worthy modern addition to the architectural fabric of the City. It might just be a masterpiece.'

The Secretary of State's approval of the Stirling building, on the recommendation of his inspector, was briefly overturned when SAVE went to the Court of Appeal. But the House of Lords reversed the court's decision and the fight was over. The fate of Mappin & Webb and the other buildings was sealed, even though the 1990 property slump delayed the start of demolition work until within days of the planning permission expiring in June 1994. Tragically, James Stirling died before construction could begin. His 'masterpiece' would be a posthumous one, carried forward by his partner Michael Wilford.

Aerial view of the site in the summer of 1994 following the demolition of the Victorian buildings between Poultry (top) and Queen Victoria Street (bottom). The medieval lanes of Bucklersbury and Pancras Lane are still present on the western side of the site but not for much longer

1 Poultry is finally built

Reactions to the new building at Poultry have been many and varied, with champions and detractors of modern architecture weighing in.

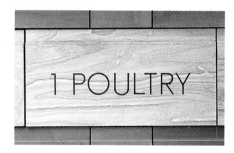

Supporters of the new building have pointed out that James Stirling was one of Britain's three most influential modernist architects, along with Norman Foster and Richard Rogers. The 1997 edition of the Pevsner Buildings of England series describes Stirling's building as a 'hard-edged and strongly articulated design' which has already influenced many other architects. It is essentially geometrical – a triangular site defining its base plan, and alternating triangular and circular shapes apparent in both the central rotunda and the facade lines. Despite such modernism, supporters of the building argue that its scale and bulk are in harmony with the surrounding buildings. The Stirling building's intelligent use of space has been described as 'elevating it above the commercial horde' and it is noticeable that the building includes a high ratio of public space. The first basement and ground-floor levels contain shops and public concourses, with five floors of offices above, topped by a roof garden and restaurant.

Looking down into the central rotunda from the roof garden

New versus old: the Queen Victoria Street frontage of 1 Poultry with the reconstructed remains of the Roman Temple of Mithras in the foreground

The central rotunda and its colourful finishes – a signature of James Stirling's buildings – seen here from the ground-floor public concourse

Stirling's buildings are known for their high quality and colourful finishes and 1 Poultry is no exception, using horizontal bands alternating between an Australian beige sandstone known as Helidon and a red sandstone from Gloucestershire called Wilderness Red. On the north facade of the building Joseph Kremer's original terracotta panels, above the entrance to the central rotunda, augment the scheme. The overall effect of the sandstone, combined with the segmentation of the facades, is impressive although many people feel that it clashes with the Portland Stone facades of many of its neighbours. Some harbour doubts about the end turret and Pevsner questions whether it can stand the test of time in the way that the Mappin & Webb turret undoubtedly did.

Only time will tell how well the new building fills its focal site and whether it can become a cherished London landmark.

Detail of Joseph Kremer's terracotta panels, dating from 1875 and showing the processions of four monarchs through the City, which was salvaged from 12–13 Poultry and re-erected as part of a frieze on the north side of the new building

1 Poultry viewed from Bank junction, with Stirling's clock turret echoing the Mappin & Webb treatment of the same prominent location 100 years earlier

12 London's archaeologists and the Walbrook

Archaeologists have been attracted to the Walbrook Valley for at least two centuries, their attempts to wrest an understanding of London's past from the ground ranging from the foolhardy to the heroic.

Pioneers

In 1724 William Stukeley produced this map of Roman London. Although remarkable for its time, a great deal more has been learned since then

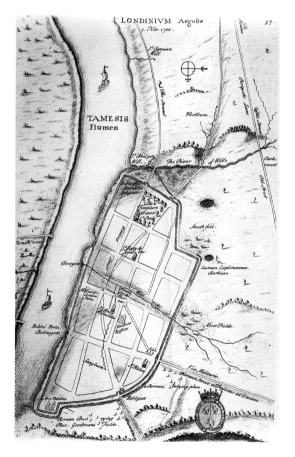

London's antiquity was recognised long before archaeologists began digging in the Walbrook Valley. The Venerable Bede referred to the abandoned Roman city when writing in the 8th century, and Roman London's defensive wall and other ruins remained in plain view up to the medieval period. The origins of London have sometimes been the subject of exaggeration and misinterpretation. Geoffrey of Monmouth's *History of the Kings of Britain*, completed around 1136, describes London as founded by the mythical figure of Brutus in about 1108 BC. Brutus was said to have brought a remnant of the Trojan race to England, which was uninhabited at the time except for a few giants, and here he founded New Troy, later known as London. At the end of the 16th century John Stow made the same spurious association between London and the ancient classical city of Troy. More careful accounting of archaeological facts slowly developed in the 17th and 18th centuries, with the recovery of artefacts from diggings in the City of London increasingly noted and described. Sir Christopher Wren recorded Roman pottery and animal bones during the rebuilding of St Paul's and observed gravel road surfaces at St Mary le Bow associated with the main east–west Roman road more recently recorded at Poultry. In 1724 William Stukeley collated these observations to produce his map of Roman London.

As the City grew, so the amount of excavation work for sewers and basements increased and with it came new discoveries. By the mid 19th century so many 'antiquities and curiosities' had been dug up or dredged up that they scarcely fitted into the Guildhall Library, and the City began to consider arranging the artefacts in cases. Throughout the 19th century archaeological discovery was driven by private collectors who recovered individual artefacts from excavations. Important finds were often purchased or picked off spoil heaps, and it was not always clear exactly where they had come from. This began to change as Charles Roach Smith established himself as the foremost collector of his time and the first outspoken defender of London's heritage.

Roach Smith sold his collection to the British Museum in 1854 and retired to the countryside, but he had provided a base for those who followed. Among these was Colonel Augustus Henry Lane-Fox (later General Pitt-Rivers), a soldier who became involved in field archaeology through an interest in Darwinian theories of evolution. Pitt-Rivers correctly recognised finds from the Upper Walbrook as Roman but, influenced by the discovery of prehistoric stilt buildings on Lake Geneva in 1854, misinterpreted the timber piles along the Walbrook as the remains of an Iron Age settlement built over a marsh. The theory that London began as a Celtic lake village would take some time to be finally disproved, but Pitt-Rivers' careful recording work was the start of a scientific approach to archaeology.

Charles Roach Smith's collection of London antiquities on display at 5 Liverpool Street in 1850

By 1869, when the Bucklersbury mosaic was discovered in Queen Victoria Street, the situation had improved to the extent that J E Price was given time to accurately measure and record the findings, and the mosaic was carefully lifted and removed to the Guildhall Library for display. Shortly afterwards Price was able to recover an assemblage of Roman tools and metalwork from the National Safe Deposit Company site nearby.

The *Illustrated London News* of 1869 recorded the discovery of the Bucklersbury mosaic in Queen Victoria Street. An estimated 50,000 people gathered to look at it over the space of three days

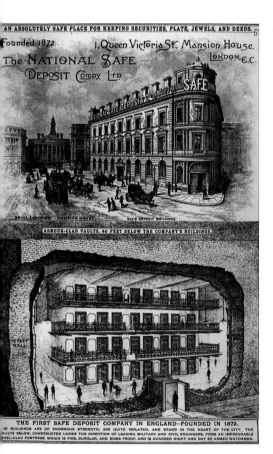

An 1880s' advertisement for the new National Safe Deposit Company building. Flooding from the Walbrook made the vaults even more secure by turning the surrounding corridor into a moat

The arrival of Mortimer Wheeler at the London Museum in 1926 was the catalyst for a dramatic advance, and Wheeler was asked to produce an overview of Roman London for the Royal Commission on Historical Monuments, published in 1928. Wheeler reconsidered Pitt-Rivers' interpretation of timbers from the Walbrook Valley and correctly identified them as Roman revetments and buildings along the banks of the stream.

Antiquities recovered during excavations for the National Safe Deposit Company building at 1 Queen Victoria Street in 1870 and displayed at the old Guildhall Museum. The deep basement lay on the site of the Roman bridge across the Walbrook stream

During the Second World War nearly a third of the City of London was destroyed by enemy bombing. The area to the south and west of Poultry was extremely hard hit, presenting archaeologists with an unprecedented opportunity to excavate sites after the war. In 1945 W F Grimes was appointed to supervise work in London and formed the Roman and Mediaeval London Excavation Council. Money and labour for excavation was in extremely short supply, but another commodity precious to archaeologists – time on site – was plentiful, as many bomb sites lay silent, with little prospect of immediate redevelopment. In 1949 the first really large redevelopment took place along the east side of the Walbrook at St Swithin's House. That winter, Ivor Noël Hume, self-described failed playwright, faced the bulldozers pretty much single-handedly, carrying artefacts back to the Guildhall Museum in sodden paper bags or, if too numerous, in a coalsack on his back or a wheelbarrow he begged off the builders. Publicity about his findings and the desperate conditions helped to convince the Corporation of London to provide more funding.

Professor W F Grimes directing the excavation of the Temple of Mithras, discovered at Bucklersbury House in 1954. As in 1869, large crowds gathered to see the finds

Grimes's greatest achievement was the excavation of the Temple of Mithras in September 1954, discovered on a large bomb site to the south of Poultry, where he had cut a trench to record the Walbrook stream. When the marble head of Mithras was uncovered on what was supposed to be the last day of the dig, the site became a *cause célèbre*. Grimes was on the site with the permission of the owners and the understanding that no delay would be caused to construction work. Ralph Merrifield of the Guildhall Museum would later say: 'If you wish to see building contractors cower and property developers turn pale, you need only whisper the words "Temple of Mithras".' Tens of thousands of people visited the site – on the last day the queue to see the temple was estimated to be a mile long and hundreds were turned away when darkness fell. Grimes described the situation as creating 'an atmosphere of excitement amounting at times to something approaching hysteria – not the most suitable one in which to conduct an orderly investigation'. Calls were made for the preservation of the remains where they stood, but the costs would have been massive. A compromise allowed the temple to be moved to the northern edge of the site, and the finds were donated to the Guildhall Museum. Most of the archaeology at Bucklersbury House was destroyed without record, though. Given the lack of time, funding or legions of trained archaeologists, it was never going to be possible to record the many hundreds of Roman timber buildings which covered the rest of the site.

'To the Temple of Mithras' – a 1954 drawing by Fougasse (Kenneth Bird) provides a perfect and ironic view of the massive public interest in the discovery

Archaeological skills today include not only careful excavation but surveying and a variety of scientific sampling techniques

Archaeologists at work in 1987 on London's deepest recorded archaeological sequence – at the site of a DLR ventilation shaft in Bucklersbury. Archaeologists did all the digging and recording themselves, while construction workers provided a crane and watched from the top – a reversal of roles from the era of Roach Smith and Pitt-Rivers when the archaeologists watched workmen dig and picked the bits off the spoil heap later

Archaeology comes of age

The 1954 furore caused by the Temple of Mithras made some developers reluctant to grant archaeologists access to their sites. At the same time the pace of development continued to quicken, and more archaeology was destroyed. A growing understanding that London's archaeology was a valuable and finite resource led to increasingly vocal demands that more should be done to protect and record it. This culminated in the 1973 publication of *The Future of London's Past*, which proposed the formation of an archaeological unit for London. Later in the year the Department of Urban Archaeology (DUA) was formed specifically to carry out archaeological research and rescue excavations supported by public funding.

During the 1970s and 1980s the Museum of London's DUA carried out a large number of excavations in the City. Archaeologists became adept at securing private funding, even though there was seldom any obligation on landowners to pay for excavation work. Each new dig added another piece to the jigsaw of evidence for Roman and medieval London. Around Poultry the opportunities for excavation were rare as little redevelopment took place. Finally, in 1987–8 construction of the Docklands Light Railway City Extension resulted in two small but important excavations at Lothbury and Bucklersbury, in advance of the construction of ventilation shafts. The excavation at Bucklersbury allowed detailed recording of London's deepest archaeological sequence – nearly 8 metres of strata dating from the founding of Roman London before AD 50 up to the Great Fire.

Modern archaeological work in the Walbrook involves teamwork, and has become less reliant on the sort of larger-than-life figures active in the area in the past. Since 1990, developers have had new obligations placed on them to fund appropriate amounts of archaeological work, and it is essential that research aims and strategies are agreed in advance of a dig. Archaeology has also had to adapt to competition in the market place, with different archaeological contractors offering their services. As a relatively small and young profession, archaeology has struggled to come to terms with these changes, particularly as it is sometimes difficult to point to tangible results and the benefits of good archaeological work.

Although the careers and experiences of members of the archaeological team at 1 Poultry were very different from those of the archaeologists who worked on sites such as the Temple of Mithras, both groups shared the knowledge that archaeological work is as much a vocation as a job. End-of-site team photographs say a lot, and the 50 diggers on site at the end of the excavation at Poultry show a sense of satisfaction and pride that a challenge has been answered.

Office life for the archaeologist has changed radically since Grimes's day, with information technology, shared databases and digital mapping systems allowing more detailed analysis than ever before. In addition to this general book, the collaborative work between all of the people involved in the project will result in three academic publications – devoted to the Roman and medieval findings, and the burial ground of St Benet Sherehog – which will appear over the next few years.

The excavation at Poultry required a large back-office for checking paperwork, processing samples and sorting and studying the large numbers of finds. Half of all the work involved in understanding the findings took place either off the site or after the digging was complete

The end-of-site photograph at Poultry – an archaeological tradition: 50 archaeologists stand on the south side of the main Roman road below the new building

Glossary

Amphora Large (7 gallon capacity), two-handled pottery vessel for storage and transport of liquids, especially wine

Apse Semicircular end of a room in a building

Arcade Series of arches supported by piers or columns

Chancel Part of a church near the altar, usually enclosed and reserved for the clergy

Dendrochronology A method of dating a timber by matching the widths of its annual growth rings with a calibrated master curve to give the felling date of a tree

Forum The civic centre in a Roman town and incorporating the municipal council, courts and market

Hypocaust Roman underfloor heating system

Insula A block of houses in a Roman town

Lollardy Act of following the 14th-century heretic named Wyclif, devoted to piety (from Dutch lollaerd meaning mumbler)

Messuage A medieval legal term for a dwelling and its associated land

Portico A colonnade forming a covered passage or gallery around a (Roman) building

Revetment A vertical structure, usually built of timber, to retain land upslope

Strata Successive layers of material deposited over time

Tenement Property containing several dwellings

Terrace A natural or manmade horizontal ground surface

Timber-framing Method of construction where the structural frame is built of interlocking timbers and the spaces between are infilled with non-structural material such as wattle and daub

Via decumana (Decumanus) The main street running east–west in a Roman town and meeting the main north–south street at the forum

Walbrook A small stream which divided Roman London in two, flowing from the area north of Moorgate and Liverpool Street Station to join the River Thames at Dowgate

Further reading

Peter Ackroyd, *Hawksmoor*, 1985

J Bird, M Hassall & II Sheldon (eds), *Interpreting Roman London*, 1996

Simon Bradley & Nikolaus Pevsner, *London I: the City of London*, The Buildings of England, 1997

C Brooke & G Keir, *London 800–1216: the shaping of a city*, 1975

Daniel Defoe, *A journal of the plague year*, 1722

Goscinny & Uderzo, *Asterix in Britain*, 1966

W F Grimes, *The excavation of Roman and mediaeval London*, 1968

Michael Hunter (ed), *Preserving the past: the rise of heritage In modern Britain*, 1996

Robert Latham (ed), *Samuel Pepys: the shorter Pepys*, 1985

Ralph Merrifield, *The Roman city of London*, 1965

Nick Merriman, *Prehistoric London*, 1990

Martin Millett, *The romanization of Britain*, 1990

Donald J Olsen, *The growth of Victorian London*, 1976

Dominic Perring, *Roman London*, 1991

John Schofield, *The building of London from the conquest to the Great Fire*, 1984

John Shepherd, *The Temple of Mithras*, 1998

Francis Sheppard, *The treasury of London's past*, 1991

John Stow, *The survey of London*, 1598 (ed C L Kingsford, 1908)

Alan Vince, *Saxon London: an archaeological investigation*, 1990

Maureen Waller, *1700 – Scenes from London life*, 2000

B Weinreb & C Hibbert, *The London encyclopaedia*, 1983

Gavin Weightman & Steve Humphries, *The making of modern London 1815–1914*, 1983

A N Wilson, *The Faber book of London*, 1993

Late Saxon bone needles from Poultry would have been used in textile-making or other weaving

Index

Page nos in bold refer to illustrations

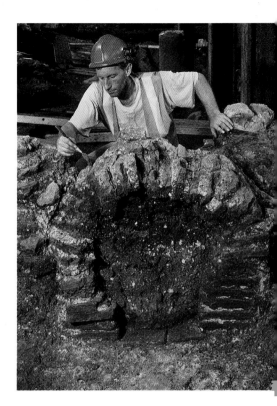

A tile arch in the east wall of the possible Roman bath building was part of a system of flues associated with underfloor heating

I suggested a doubt, that if I were to reside
in London, the exquisite zest with which I
relished it in occasional visits might go off,
and I might grow tired of it.

JOHNSON: 'Why, Sir, you find no man, at all
intellectual, who is willing to leave London.
No, Sir, when a man is tired of London, he is
tired of life; for there is in London all that
life can afford.'

James Boswell, *Life of Johnson*
20 September 1777

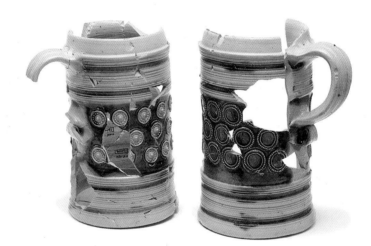

Late 17th-century imported tankards, made of
salt-glazed stoneware with cobalt blue decoration,
had been thrown into a household rubbish pit
near Bucklersbury

Peter Rowsome led the Museum of London's excavations at Poultry and is involved in continuing research and publication of the results. He has supervised several important excavations concerning Roman and medieval London, as well as digs in Italy and the Middle East, and is a Senior Project Manager at the Museum of London Archaeology Service.

The author is grateful to the following institutions and individuals for permission to reproduce illustrations on the pages indicated: Martin Bentley (27); Judith Dobie, English Heritage Centre for Archaeology (19, 25, 41, 51); © 2000 Les Editions Albert Rene / Goscinny-Uderzo (34, 35); Peter Froste (16, 31, 46); The Guardian Newspaper Ltd (80); Guildhall Art Gallery, Corporation of London (5); Guildhall Library, Corporation of London (44, 57, 66, 70, 72, 73, 74, 76, 77, 79, 86); Peter Jackson (58); Kansas State Historical Society (21); Macmillan Children's Books, London (71); Museo Archeologico Nazionale, Naples, Italy/Bridgeman Art Library (32); © National Monuments Record (74, 76); National Monuments Record, English Heritage (75); Lord Palumbo (80); John Pearson (9, for Cultural Heritage Resources 49); SAVE Britain's Heritage (80); Richard Sorrell (23). All other images are Museum of London Archaeology Service / Museum of London.